Professional Selling

A JOURNEY, NOT A DESTINATION

Frank Salisbury

OAK·TREE·PRESS

Published by
OAK TREE PRESS
19 Rutland Street, Cork, Ireland
www.oaktreepress.com

A catalogue record of this book is
available from the British Library.

ISBN 978 1 904887 76 8 (Paperback)
ISBN 978 1 904887 77 5 (ePub)
ISBN 978 1 904887 79 9 (Kindle)

CONTENTS

FIGURES

TABLES

ACKNOWLEDGEMENTS

Particular thanks are due to Dawn Metcalfe for reviewing and correcting the material in this book and for suggesting improvements.

PREFACE

How to succeed in selling is as difficult to fathom as life itself. People are complicated and their personalities are complex. If anyone tells you that they have the secret of success in selling, smell their breath. It could be just that I am getting older. However, I would like to think that age has brought with it a certain amount of valuable and relevant experience and that I have not become the sort of person who used to annoy me by saying, "It wasn't like this in my day". I have to say, though, "It *wasn't* like this in my day" – selling, that is.

Professional selling, as an activity, seems to have disappeared. Whether it is shopping for electrical goods, furniture, or garden equipment, or listening to people trying to sell you double-glazing, insurance, or politics, the experience is the same – nobody seems to listen, nobody seems to care, and nobody seems to have any of the skills of the professional salesperson.

Even buying something as simple as a picture frame is frustrating. The other day I called into one of the increasing number of picture frame franchises springing up all over the place to get a clip frame for a print I bought in Barcelona some time ago. I waited while the assistant finished making her coffee under the counter. "I've been trying all morning to make this", she said. "I haven't had a break all day (it was only 11 a.m.) and, customers or not, I'm determined to have a cup of coffee". I should have taken it as a warning and left – however, I continue to have this forlorn belief that poor customer service has more to do with my unrealistic expectations than the lack of sales skills in shop assistants. I ignored the tragic story of overwork and lack of caffeine. "I'm looking for a clip frame to fit this, please". "Have you looked over there?" she said – and so it went on. I left the shop without the clip frame I wanted. In the end, I went to a specialist framer, who charged me a small fortune to make a frame that matched the print. I had used the specialist before. I knew he was expensive, but this print was not exactly a Picasso and I had set out originally for something cheap and cheerful.

I had disobeyed one of my own primary sales rules: 'You get what you pay for'. The craftsman, for that is what the specialist is, convinced me that, if I put a good frame on the print, it would enhance my enjoyment and fit in with others he had framed for me previously. He was right. It also enhanced his pocket. Having said that, he is the sort of person who does not have to look for work – it comes to him. He is good. He is also a very good salesman, although he neither knows it nor admits it – which is a common trait displayed by most of the successful salespeople and businesspeople I know. They are unaware of their sales skills, putting their success down mainly to hard work. In observing them, however, they display common traits, behaviours, and actions. In this book, I hope to share some of those traits with you.

I like dealing with people who appear to care about what they sell you. However, in the shop on the high street, I wanted to buy; not only did the assistant fail to sell, but I was also put off buying. That is what I mean about today. There seem to be many more instances of me being put off buying than was the case in the past – or is it just age?

A great disappointment to me is that there are too many salespeople, and far too many companies, who believe that selling can be learned in two days. This does not stop companies running two-day sales courses and expecting people to perform instantly thereafter. Only the other day, I was discussing with a senior training manager the sales training needs he had. When he started with "I'm always interested in seeing new sales techniques and processes", I knew I was in trouble. At that stage, I ignored my second sales rule and told him what I thought, which was not what he wanted to hear. I told him that the answer to sales success lies within the behaviour of those who are already successful in the company, not with me.

The problem with me is that I am becoming increasingly intolerant of amateurs. Perhaps it is indeed a function of age. It is also, I suppose, a function of confidence in my own ability and the success that it has brought. I do not need to deal with people who do not want to deal with me. I recall a successful colleague of mine who said to me a great many years ago, "I do not sell to people who do not want to buy from me. Therefore, I assume, before I visit anybody, that they all want to buy from me". I agree with the sentiment and, having adopted that sort of attitude on many occasions, I have found it most successful.

People like dealing with confident salespeople, and the more you give the impression that you are not bothered, the more it seems to attract people. In the case of this particular training manager, I was too bothered. I tried to teach him in five minutes, which was the level of attention he gave to the subject, what had taken me a lifetime to learn. I should have walked away there and then. It did me no favours trying to sell him something he simply could not understand – and this is a point worth learning for everyone considering a professional career in selling.

The most important person in the sales process is you. You have to live with yourself after the sale, whether it is successful or not. I have read a lot about the need to be customer-focussed and I agree that this is a critical function of the sales process, but it is not as critical as the focus on your own professional attitude. Professionals in all occupations are focussed on self: self-esteem, self-analysis, and self-preservation. The way in which you perform the sales role must enhance your self-esteem. You must be able to analyse your performance in terms of the professional image you want to attain and display. You must be able to cope with the potential rejection that exists in selling and to protect yourself from the doubts that can creep into your self-esteem whenever you appear to be going through a bad patch. All salespeople go through bad patches. The measure of success in selling is probably more to do with how you cope with failure than how you achieve and cope with success. Coping with success is easy. Coping with failure is difficult. Yet the fact is that everyone in the world has bad times as well as good times, it is just that the bad times stay with you more than the good times. Someone once asked me, "How many times do you need to hear 'Yes' before you get over a 'No'?" The ratio is probably 10 to 1.

If you are looking for the answer to sales success in some miracle technique or phrase in this book, then you may be disappointed. As I told the training manager, the answer to sales success lies within.

It may not be in fashion these days but, for most, if not all, of this book, I have attempted to keep it simple. Although I have included references to Neuro Linguistic Programming (NLP) and Emotional Intelligence and the like, I do so merely to avoid being accused of ignoring them and for the sake of completeness.

Whenever I am asked to help companies analyse their sales training needs, I do not approach the task as though it was a precursor to writing a paper on nuclear fusion. To me, sales training is a simple matter of deciding what the company wants to say to the customer and teaching the sales team to consistently:

- Say it.
- Improve it.
- Sound and look convincing whilst they are saying it.

I truly believe that if you get any more complicated than this, then you might have lost the plot.

In this book, I talk about 'the professional game of selling'. I have spent a lot of time over the last few years comparing sports with selling. Like many people in selling, I have attended sales conferences and seminars where sporting analogies and images were used to elicit some motivation amongst the audience. In common with most in the audience, and all those presenting, I was unable to apply those analogies in the 'real world', as salespeople and managers are liable to call it. Few of us can recall pole vaulting into the office, and the last time we did 100 metres in less than 10 seconds was when the Regional Sales Manager came calling.

Yet, when I really began to understand how athletes become professional, I realised that the truth had been staring me in the face all the time. In addition, the same evidence exists in the professions of acting, dancing and music. Hopefully, the section on the professional game of selling will be as much a revelation to you as it was to me.

It is within this premise that I set out my stall deliberately to challenge you to question everything you have ever known or held dear about selling and professionalism. I think that selling is an honourable profession practised by many amateurs. It is about time that we realised that selling is a physical skill, which requires salespeople, sales managers, and sales trainers alike to apply the simple processes of repetition and hard work, in order to have a successful outcome.

I do not believe in closing techniques or in overcoming objections, although again I have included both for the sake of completeness. The same applies to the learning of differences between open and closed questions, and listening skills.

This book does not contain the answers to sales success. It merely contains the background reading material. Having said that, contrary to popular belief, selling is a well researched and recorded activity and the bookshops and libraries are full of books, articles, and research papers covering every aspect of selling. You just need to know where to look.

Last, the book should be viewed as part of the process of self-discovery. It is through self-awareness of who we are, what we want to be, and what the barriers are to our potential success that we can begin to tackle those barriers in order to achieve the potential that lies within us all.

Frank Salisbury
Joint Founder, Institute of Professional Selling
July 2011
Dublin

Part One
THE BASICS OF
PROFESSIONAL SELLING

CHAPTER 1

THE HISTORY OF SELLING

SUMMARY

- It is important to accept that selling has and continues to have a bad press.

- Selling, if it is anything, is about communication. Communication means having a common language. If you concur that most people are suspicious of salespeople and their motives, then you have begun a common understanding with the customer.

- You can take comfort from the fact that selling is an honourable profession. Without selling as an activity, most organisations would grind to a halt. This goes for both commercial and non-profit making organisations.

SELLING: IN THE BEGINNING

It was Robert Louis Stevenson who said, "Everything in life is selling" and, whether you define selling as being the act of trading, bartering or simply exchanging goods or services, it is obvious that it has been with us a long time. In fact, selling as an activity has existed for thousands of years. As far back as 4000 BC, merchants were travelling the length and breadth of the Tigris and Euphrates rivers, and trading their goods. Whether selling involves this exchange of goods for complementary goods and services, or eventually for common currency, it is certain that we appear always to have sold to each other. In a sense then, selling has existed in symmetry with the evolution of the human race, owing to the fact that we are all essentially salespeople from the minute we are born into society. Children are salespeople in so much as they practise the art of persuasion on their parents, and later their schoolteachers and peers. As the years progress, we employ these techniques in situations such as college and job interviews. Nowadays, you will be hard pressed to find a profession that has no selling capacity involved in it:

> The modern marketing concept now embodied in the management philosophies of most leading corporations claims that all business is selling.[1]

Despite the fact that selling has always been with us, the actual process of selling has never enjoyed a good press. The ancient Roman word for salesman meant 'cheater' and, in *The Republic*, Plato made his views on salespeople quite clear:

> Suppose now, that a businessman, or an artisan, brings some production to market, and he comes at a time when there is no one to exchange with him – is he to leave his calling and sit idle in the market place? Not at all, he will find people there who, seeing the want, undertake the office of salesman. In well-ordered states, they are commonly those who are the weakest in bodily strength, and therefore of little use for any other purposes.

This was written at a time when the two main professions were farming and soldiering. The army conquered and maintained the empire, and farmers fed the army. Salespeople intervened in this process and made money from transporting grain to the army.

It could be argued that the sole purpose of conquest has always been trade. The early traders were not strictly what we would call salespeople, because they and their families produced most of the goods they were trading. They worked on a process of material logistics, as opposed to personal selling.

But, whether anyone likes the fact or not, we are all in selling. Everyone is trying to sell somebody else something.

---

[1]   Russell, F., Beach, F., Buskirk, R. and Buskirk, B. (1988). *Selling Principles and Practices*, 12th edition, New York: McGraw-Hill.

THE INDUSTRIAL REVOLUTION AND SELLING

In Europe, associations known as guilds came to dominate trading in the early part of the Middle Ages and provided a framework for the beginnings of industrialised nations. Contemporary equivalent organisations may be business associations or institutes.

Salespeople, in the true sense of the word, are said to have emerged in the late 1700s, pre-dating the Industrial Revolution. The first evidence of a significant sales force points to Manchester and its textile industry, hence the use of 'Manchester Man' as a term for a salesman. As they had no ownership interest in the companies they were selling for, arguably these were the first *bona fide* salespeople. As these salespeople marketed their goods from bags of samples, they quickly became known as 'bagmen'. This method of selling required a shift in buyer attitudes, as consumers could not personally verify the quality of the merchandise and had to trust that the sample fairly represented the product that would be delivered following purchase. Consumers' concerns at this time focused more on the quality of the goods as opposed to deceitful sales techniques.

In America, these earliest salespeople were known as 'greeters', as they would visit the hotels where retailers were staying to ask for business for the variety of suppliers for whom they worked. As the development of the railroads facilitated easier travel, these salespeople were able to travel to the traders' actual workplaces and so the term 'greeter' came to be replaced by 'drummer'. Apart from the obvious explanation for this (the salespeople beat a drum to announce their arrival), it is also suggested that this name stemmed from the vast trunks that the salespeople carried around, known as drums. The public usually (and often rightly) were suspicious of the drummers, and the notoriety they earned during this period for their often highly immoral sales methods forms the basis for a great deal of today's banter about 'travelling salespeople' and opposition to heavy-handed sales techniques.

By the end of the 19th century, the UK and European subsidiaries of Australian and Canadian life assurance companies began to establish large sales forces, paid by commission on policies sold rather than by regular salary. It was these sales forces, in particular, that developed techniques for closing and overcoming objections, which replaced the more genteel process of buying life assurance from local life assurance companies whose sales efforts depended on part-time agents, many of whom were in the acceptable professions of accountancy, law and banking. In fact, such part-time professional agents are still prevalent in countries such as France and Germany, where the image of insurance salespeople appears to be less tarnished than is the case elsewhere. Nonetheless, the idea that someone can make a living only by making a sale is something that many people cannot come to terms with and contributes to the general mistrust of salespeople, especially those who call at one's home.

In the 20th century, selling changed radically, from playing second fiddle to manufacturing, as industrialisation brought with it superior methods of production, resulting in an excess of goods and the emergence of a buyer's market. This prompted a renewed interest in selling and the sales process, and led to what is commonly referred to as the era of the modern drummer. Despite this, sales techniques did not change greatly, as drummers relied heavily on canned presentations, first introduced by John H. Patterson of National Cash Registers (NCR). Then, just before the Second World War, as the Great Depression of the 1930s shattered the framework of the American free enterprise system, companies began to use marketing personnel to carry out tasks such as market research.

Around 1948, the situation began to stabilise, bringing about what has been referred to as the modern sales era, in which the philosophy of the marketing concept began to emerge. Consequently, salespeople ostensibly became more professional, owing to the sales support mechanisms that were being built up behind them by their organisations.

This changed further in the 1970s, as emphasis was placed on the salesperson as a problem-solver, in the sense that the salesperson should be able to meet the buyer's needs, as opposed to merely selling them merchandise.[2]

---

[2]   Johnson, E.M., Kurtz, D.L. and Scheuing, E.E. (1987). *Sales Management,* New York: McGraw-Hill.

SALESPEOPLE'S IMAGE

Whilst selling as an activity is viewed by many as the engine through which the economy has grown over the last two centuries, for others the image of the salesperson remains tarnished. Everyone has a story about being sold something they did not really want. Yet most people also have bought something from carefully considered choice that was equally unwanted, or ultimately a waste of money. However, self-critical stories of our useless buying decisions are less comfortable to relate.

In an article published some time ago,[3] it was said that:

> Salespeople's primary motivation is an amalgam of greed and hostility, with hostility directed principally toward their supervision, and toward the public to whom they sell.

The author was referring to comments made by some unknown writer, but the point has been repeated in various other forms across a number of other journals.

It is very clear that most people have a poor image of salespeople. One report[4] showed that nearly 30% of all potential buyers of financial services products were put off buying by the attitude displayed by the salesperson, while only 25% had decided to buy an investment product after meeting a salesperson.

Surveys regularly show that people are less than trusting of salespeople. Yet strangely, in most companies, salespeople are the single most important link with the customer. For many customers, the salesperson *is* the company. However, even within those same companies, being a salesperson is rarely seen as a worthwhile career: a commonly-held belief is that, if you have talent, then it might be wasted in sales.

---

[3] Jolson, M.A. (1989). 'Canned adaptiveness: A new direction for modern salesmanship', *Business Horizons*, January-February.

[4] LIMRA (1998). *Purchasing Patterns for Life and Pensions Products*, Windsor, CT: LIMRA.

IS SELLING A PROFESSION?

Perhaps selling is not a profession in the true sense. There are professionals who practice selling but it could be that, without a considerable change in both mindset and approach, selling will not be viewed as a profession.

Yet, in the same way that some would argue that sports is not a profession, there are professional sportspeople. Apart from classical music, music itself may not be classed as a profession, although there are professional musicians. Apart from ballet, dancing in general may not be a profession, yet there are professional dancers. Acting? Acting is seen as a profession, which is strange. Actors become professional in very much the same way as sportspeople, dancers, and musicians, and yet appear to have more kudos than these counterparts.

Why mention these professionals whilst at the same time talking about selling? It is because I believe that selling could be the same. It is a physical skill, and mastery of that skill through similar methodologies used by sportspeople, dancers, musicians, and actors can bring about the professionalism we desire.

MARKETING *VS* SELLING

It may be that a hybrid of the selling industry – marketing – has some responsibility for the poor image of salespeople. Marketing is supposed to meet the needs of customers by offering products that the customer needs at the right price, by persuasion and promotion in the right place at a profit: these are known as the six 'Ps' of marketing. Some people, in the true tradition of marketing, have reduced these to the four 'Ps' – namely price, promotion, place, and profit, usually called the marketing mix – thereby giving a 30% discount!

The role of the salesperson is to persuade the customer to buy, whereas marketing is used to provide products and services the customers need – or so those in marketing would have you believe.

Ken Clark[5] mentions Theodore Levitt's views on selling from the *Harvard Business Review* in 1975:

> Selling focuses on the needs of the seller, marketing on the needs of the buyer. Selling is preoccupied with the seller's need to convert his product into cash; marketing is concerned with the idea of satisfying the needs of the customer by means of the product, and the whole cluster of things associated with creating, delivering and finally consuming it. In short, the organisation must learn to think of itself not as producing goods or services, but as buying customers, as doing the things that will make people want to do business with it.

Definitions of selling and marketing

Kotler[6] defines marketing as:

> Human activity directed at satisfying needs and wants through exchange processes.

In a sellers' marketplace, Kotler said that it is the salesperson who has the power, as though buying and selling is some kind of conflict process. The selling concept, he says:

> ... holds that consumers will not buy enough of the organisation's products unless the organisation undertakes a substantial selling and promotion effort.

So there we have it. Marketing is a case of customers buying. Selling, it appears, involves some kind of process that ultimately foists goods and services on people, who left to their own devices, would not normally have bought them. It would be wrong not to admit that this foisting happens, for it does. Equally, however, there are far more salespeople trying to provide their customers with something they believe in and something that will benefit both supplier and consumer. For these and other reasons, even salespeople themselves

5   Clark, K. (1991). *Blueprint for Life: How to Survive and Prosper in the Life Assurance Business*, Ipswich: K.C. Promotions.
6   Kotler, P. (1983). *Principles of Marketing*, Englewood Cliffs, N.J.: Prentice Hall International.

are keen to distance themselves from the term 'sales' or 'selling' in their own job titles.

I define selling as:

1. Identifying qualified buyers who will purchase your product or service.

2. Selling yourself and your company's image to those potential buyers through a process of identification of needs and wants.

3. Agreeing upon a course of action that is profitable to both parties.

Why has marketing, with such a short history, succeeded in being recognised as a profession, and selling, which is what all of us were doing, remained largely unrecognised? I think that Francis,[7] writing about quality and selling, may have had part of the answer when he said:

> ... wherever there is a lack of empirical knowledge or research, myths and demi-gods flourish.

Sadly, this is exactly what has happened in the selling profession. However, my own findings show that, far from there being a lack of serious research into selling, there is a surfeit. The problem is that, for some reason, it does not reach educational establishments. Even more curious is that I know of only a handful of sales trainers who have conducted any cursory – let alone empirical – research into selling. This has left the profession open to peddlers of quack sales mythologies and hyped conferences where followers are expected to pay homage to the latest white-suited sales prophet.

THINGS ARE CHANGING

The reality of the commercial world and global competition mean that selling as an activity and a profession is probably more important now than it ever has been. Whether people at the front end of the sales process call themselves salespeople or marketing executives, my belief is that they are in sales. I also note that most

---

[7]   Francis, K. (1993). *TQM in Sales and Marketing: A Practitioner's Guide*, Letchworth: Technical Communication (Publishing) Ltd.

people these days are involved in sales – whether in Customer Relationship Management, Key Account Management or any hybrid of these. In addition, it is not unusual for salespeople to be generally highly-qualified individuals. Possessing a third-level degree can be an asset in many sales environments. In certain industries and market sectors (for example, engineering, IT, government supplies, accountancy practices, etc), having a good educational background is often a basic criterion for employment in the first place. It is my hope that a qualification in sales also will be seen as an entry requirement for a career in selling.

NEXT ...

- Ask people you know to name some professions. How often is 'selling' mentioned? Probably, hardly at all. Why is this?
- Draw up two lists: one of positive words associated with salespeople and one of negative words associated with salespeople. Are there any conclusions you can draw from this?
- How do you think the image of salespeople could be improved in order to make it a positive career choice?

CHAPTER 2

BECOMING A PROFESSIONAL SALESPERSON

SUMMARY

- If selling was viewed as a professional game, we might be more willing to adopt an inflexible set of rules towards it.

- All professionals use scripts. Far from suppressing personality, the use of scripts is an enabling factor in performance. The only people who sound as if they are using a script are those who have not practised sufficiently.

- A failure to choose selling as a career early in our development means that we probably do not appreciate the processional processes involved in acquiring, maintaining and improving our sales skills.

- The coach needs to observe your performance and to provide you with feedback.

- A common trait in all professionals is the constant desire to improve.

THE PROFESSIONAL GAME OF SELLING

In this book, I talk about selling as though it might be viewed as a professional game. If I were to apply a visual to it, it might look something like **Figure 1**. At either end of the tennis court are two people – you and the customer. It is your serve.

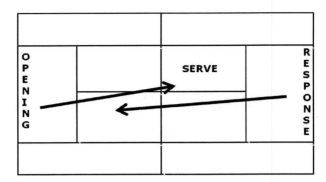

Figure 1: Selling as a Game of Tennis

The opening

As with all professions, there is an opening and it brings about a response. When a musician plays the first chords of a piece of music, they expect it to grab the audience's attention. When an actor delivers the first line of a speech in a play, they want you to sit up and listen. When you see the first scene in a dance movement, the objective is to interest you to make you want to see more.

In selling, there is a stimulus and a response. The opening few lines are meant to elicit a response from a customer that should make them want to hear more. You serve your sales proposition and the customer returns the serve by responding. Whether the return is what you expect depends upon the quality of your serve.

Using a script

A colleague of mine noted, "Isn't it amazing that salespeople will spend an inordinate amount of time preparing a speech to give in front of the boss, but spend no time at all practising what they will say in front of the customer?"

What would happen if an actor made the words up every night on the stage? What would their performance be like? What is the effect of repeating the same words night after night? It should make the delivery better. It should help the actor focus on the delivery. By focusing on the delivery instead of on the words, the performance gets better.

What would happen if a dancer made up new steps each time they went onstage? What would happen if a musician made up a new score each time they played in an orchestra? What would happen if a golfer changed the way in which they held the club each time they hit a ball?

It seems that the only people who think they get better by making it up are salespeople. The fact is that, in order to maintain consistency, in order to improve, in order to be professional, sales presentations should be scripted. The truth is that most of us in sales, whether at the sales front line, sales managers, or sales trainers, seem to have an inbuilt resistance to scripts. The usual cry is that it clones us. If cloning involves making people into professionals, then I see nothing wrong with cloning. In reality, using a script is liberating, not constricting. Ask any actor.

Flexibility and adaptiveness

Hayes and Hartley[8] proposed that salespeople must be flexible in their approach to buyers. They advocate that each industry has a unique set of rules, and that the salesperson not only must understand those rules but also realise that the individuals operating in buying functions in each of those diverse industries also are diverse in the way in which they communicate. They said:

> ... the data confirms our fundamental expectations – that it is imperative for the salesperson to make significant adjustments in his or her behaviour between calls on those in different functions.

Taking this to its logical conclusion, one almost can envisage salespeople getting into cars, pulling down the blinds, and undergoing some frightening form of metamorphosis before calling on the next buyer! Is it really possible for salespeople to change between calls? This view leads us to believe that each sales situation demands a different approach and thus that salespeople must remain flexible in their approach. However, in my experience, it is consistency, not flexibility, that makes a professional salesperson.

---

[8]   Hayes, M.H. and Hartley, S.W. (1989). 'How buyers view industrial salespeople', *Industrial Marketing Management*, May, pp.73-80.

Many top salespeople have found a way that works to get their message across, and they use it over and over again. I have yet to meet a top salesperson who is adaptive. Most top salespeople are very inflexible in both their approach and delivery of their sales message, although when questioned closely, they will strongly deny the need for structure and consistency in their sales presentation. I believe that this response is a protective cloak they wear to mystify their success: perhaps the thought that their sales success can be emulated by anyone who cares to learn from them is too much of a threat?

Professionals in every field tend to specialise. They find a way of doing something well, and repeat the process until they become better. Football teams are made up of attackers, defenders, mid-fielders, and a goalkeeper. When a goalkeeper is sent off, it sends panic through the team, and lifts the opposition's spirits. When a team needs to defend, they take attackers off, and replace them with a defender. When the lead violinist in an orchestra falls ill, the pianist does not replace them. Leading actors have stand-ins who have learned the leading part, not everyone else's. Professionals are not expected to adapt themselves to the audience or the opposition. The shape of the team may change but the individual plays to their strengths, and they are expected to play to a system.

Career choice dictates approach to professionalism
Less than 1% of salespeople chose selling as a career whilst at school. But, if you ask people in the professions of sport, music, dance or acting, what they wanted to be when they left school, 99% will say, "What I am now". In many cases, someone else fuelled their desire at a very early age, perhaps a parent, grandparent, guardian, teacher or any number of role models. Their career choice was not something they were born to do; it was something they grew into. The desire was developed and fashioned whilst they were more aware of their possibilities than their shortcomings. It is only later that we acquire doubts about our abilities. As children, we believe anything is possible.

The fact that these professionals chose a particular path in their lives gives them a significant edge over salespeople who have not.

They are more open to the rigours of the professional processes described below. They are less suspicious of teachers (managers, trainers, and coaches) than are salespeople. They are better team players — they understand that more can be achieved by working together with other people. They focus on the positive, not the negative — they think about success, not about failure. There are more differences than similarities with salespeople.

But all is not lost. What I have observed is that professionalism in the disciplines I examined (sports and the performing arts of dance, acting, and music) does not happen in a random manner. Whilst desire and commitment certainly play a part in professionalism, the acquisition of skill – and the translation of that skill into success – has more to do with process than with anything else. These professionals and their coaches use systematic processes in order to deliver of their best. It is these processes that I will examine in more detail.

PROFESSIONAL PROCESSES

So what are these processes? **Figure 2** shows a model that I call Professional Processes, showing the elements that many professionals adopt when seeking to acquire and display top performance.

Figure 2: The Professional Processes Model

I firmly believe that if salespeople understood, accepted and adopted these principles, that they would deliver higher performance levels than they have hitherto.

Rules

The model is focussed on rules. True professionalism comes from a starting point of accepting the rules within which the professional can perform. The first task you and your coach face is to determine the rules that apply to your sales process, for you to accept these rules, and then to apply them. There may be a time that you disagree with the coach. However, that is more your problem than the coach's problem. As a professional, sometimes you just have to get on with it: your job is to perform.

Tools

Most professionals have tools they use, and they understand that the way in which those tools are used requires compliance with basic rules. An actor knows that they must use a stage prop in a certain way at a certain time, and they know that they must stick to the script. A dancer uses a certain type of footwear specific to a particular dance style. They accept that they must perform a number of steps in a certain sequence. A guitarist knows that they must strike the strings of a guitar in a particular fashion, and hold the strings on the fret board in a certain way in order to comply with the music — which they follow.

The tools of selling might include:

- **Sales reports:** These allow you to determine your current level of performance in relation to where the coach wants you to perform.
- **Training packages:** You can use these to return to basics.
- **Sales presenters, visuals, brochures, and point-of-sale systems:** These should be used in a certain way – for example, you do not simply give a brochure to a customer to read; you take them through it, highlighting the important points you want to make. If using a particular point-of-sale system (for example, a presentation on a laptop computer) you might want to ensure that the customer sits in a certain place whilst you present.

Basic training

In order to release talent and ability, people must be able to learn and perform the basics, mostly through repetition and skill drilling. The important thing is for you to be able to determine with certainty what it is that makes up the basics. When I have watched professional coaches in other disciplines, they seem to have no problems in deciding what is involved in basic training. You and the coach must work out what is basic and what is advanced. Basic is what you are expected to be able to do and achieve as a minimum standard.

For example, a football coach will want to see that you can kick the ball in the desired direction. They do not expect to have to show you how to do that. The scout will watch you play before the club makes a move to sign you. As a professional sportsperson, you will expect to be watched playing, and to show that you can perform the basics.

Personal responsibility

You are the only person who is responsible for your personal performance. You can become better at a particular skill today than you were yesterday. For many people, however, improvement goals are usually set for tomorrow: "I'll start that diet tomorrow. As soon as I get the exercise bike. After I come back from holiday. When I've finished this packet of cigarettes". Personal effectiveness and responsibility for performance improvement only really happens when dealt with in the immediate time-scale. In order to acquire a skill, to improve a skill, or to retain a skill, there has to be desire, commitment and determination from you to do something now.

You already have a significant amount of the physical skills needed in selling. Babies do not need training to seek food. They move their heads and mouths, and seek food; these are the internal 'motor' skills, which relate to the way in which we can already, without training, perform certain physical things. This is why when some people say, "I can't do that", you almost always can translate it as "I choose not to do that". Sometimes by telling ourselves that we cannot do something, we appear to lose the ability to be able to do so. We create an innate inability – effectively, we coach ourselves to be unable to do something.

Having run hundreds of sessions with groups of salespeople to determine what basic training might apply to them, I have compiled the following list:

- **Sales selection interviews:** You should expect to be required to audition for the job.

- **Skills drills at sales meetings:** You should expect that you and your colleagues will practise your sales skills at each and every meeting.

- **Practise:** Something that every professional does. We already know most salespeople do not practise enough, which could be why only 15% to 20% of salespeople exceed target. There is no other profession where you are allowed to practise on a live audience other than in selling.

- **Structure and scripts for customer approaches and sales situations:** If you are practising what to say and how to say it, you need a structure.

- **Warm up:** Every professional returns to basics just before a performance. In sales, we hear about the need to return to basics as though it was something unusual. Make it your norm by warming up before every customer meeting.

Improvement and the coach

The coach, if you have one, cannot help you to improve until such time as you have learned and can display the basics at a consistent level. You cannot achieve consistency by constantly changing what you do. This means applying a less flexible method of selling than perhaps you are used to. In the long run, however, the work that you engage in at the beginning of your journey towards professionalism will allow more and more flexibility in approach later on, when you have passed the basic stage.

Having run hundreds of sessions with groups of salespeople to determine what generic rules might apply to them, the ones that have emerged are:

- **Practising:** You should practise your basic openings at least once a day.

- **Implementation of policies, compliance and regulatory processes:** In some industries (for example, financial services), the way in which the salesperson acts and conducts the sales process is highly regulated. You must observe the rules in this area at all times.

- **Being observed:** Your coach cannot determine how to help you improve if they do not observe you at work. You must understand and accept that this should happen regularly.

- **Learning what 'good' looks like, and copying it:** Once the coach has determined what 'good' looks like, then it is your responsibility to learn how to replicate it.

- **Consistency:** You must be able to deliver a basic performance to a basic level of competence whenever asked to do so.

- **Show the customer that you are listening:** You should be able to learn and deliver a performance based on active listening techniques.

- **A structured approach to the sales process:** Your coach may decide that he/she wants the sales process to follow a certain structure based on, for example, best practice. It is their right to demand that this is adhered to.

- **Understanding, accepting, and acting on the vision:** The organisation you work for and your coach may decide that they want you to operate in a particular market, or that you are expected to display certain ethical standards.

DESIRE TO IMPROVE

Where does desire come from? It is a trait that exists in the professionals from sports and the performing arts of music, dance and acting. In fact, my experience of working with these people is that they are almost always dissatisfied with their current performance, believing always that they can do better.

In my model, I have placed the coach between the core elements (rules, etc) and 'desire to improve' simply because, in business, I believe that we need help and constant encouragement to improve.

In addition, if normal practice dictates that our line managers rarely accompany us on sales calls, with the explicit purpose of providing us with feedback, how can we judge our progress other than by our sales figures? The fact is that sales figures, whilst being critically important to our job survival, do not tell the whole story. And they certainly do not tell how we achieved success. Because the other professionals have a systematic approach to acquiring their skills in the first place, they also use that system to maintain and improve their performance. By implication, they additionally use that process to rectify their performance if it is not producing the results they had hoped for.

One of my rules for coaches is 'we constantly improve; there is no standing still'. This should be a maxim for you also. But what is it that you want to improve? If the coach does not observe you perform on sales calls, you will be left merely with an analysis of your business results. Whilst important, they rarely tell the whole story.

ACTIVITY *VS* EFFECTIVENESS

There is a difference between activity and effectiveness. Simply seeing more people is not guaranteed to make you more successful. We know that many sales performance management systems seek to draw statistical conclusions from call rates and business achievement. The theory is that, if you conducting a number of sales exchanges with customers per day, then increasing the number of sales exchanges will increase your level of business.

The real answer to this is that 'it depends'. If 10 customer sales exchanges a day results in 10 units being sold, 20 customer exchanges will not necessarily result in 20 units being sold. Dealing with 10 customers per day might be the limit of your ability within a given time period. It could be that the process means that it is impossible to increase the number of customer exchanges without reducing the amount of time spent with each customer. Many call centre salespeople complain that they are judged on the number of calls they handle, not the quality of the call. There is a fine balance between making the customer feel that you have provided them with a quality service, and answering the telephone in the first place.

My research shows that top salespeople actually deal with marginally fewer customers per day than average-performing salespeople. What they seem to be able to do, however, is to sell more to each customer. They also appear to be able to analyse what contributes to their success and therefore to focus on improving those particular elements. On the other hand, they also appear to be able to analyse what is detracting from their success and to seek actions to reduce the influence of these elements. But remember, top salespeople represent only 10% to 15% of the sales population. It might be that we are in the other 85% to 90% of salespeople, and we could do with help. Help from the coach.

If selling is about face-to-face exchanges, or at the very least 'ear-to-ear' exchanges, then surely it is what you say, and do, that matters. Focusing on activity, as so many salespeople and managers do, is as pointless as dancers focussing on the number of steps they take, or taps within a minute. It might be clever but is it entertainment? Musicians do not concentrate on how many notes they play, but on the quality of those notes. An athlete does not focus simply on the number of miles they run every week, but in the timing of those runs. Actors do not become better simply by delivering more lines. Saying "See more people" to a salesperson is as pointless as saying "Dance more steps" to a dancer, or "Run more miles" to an athlete, or "Learn more lines" to an actor or "Play more notes" to a musician. Unless, of course, the salesperson simply is not trying.

My experience, however, is that if this is the case, then no amount of "See more people" works. The signpost for lack of effort leads to a place called 'failure' – and career change. The responsibility for effort lies with you, not with your manager.

The delivery of a performance, therefore, depends not just on effort but on how you apply that effort. To move from innate inability to conscious inability is, for many people, a momentous step. It requires you to accept that your current level of performance is your personal responsibility – and your choice to deliver at that level. Of the people who perform at a low level (innate inability), most refuse

to accept this proposition, while high performers (innate ability) sometimes take it too much for granted, and stand still.

Becoming a professional salesperson requires you to never be satisfied with your current performance. You *always* can do better.

NEXT ...

- What is it that you do that cannot be replaced by someone else or by a system?
- What did you want to become when you were at school? What did you do about it? What effect has that had on your current career?
- Why do professionals have coaches?

CHAPTER 3
WHAT MAKES A GOOD SALESPERSON?

SUMMARY

- There is no evidence to support the theory that there are specific personalities more suited to sales than others. Anyone can be taught to become successful at selling. It does require desire, however. You will never be successful at anything you do not want to do. The following are myths:
  - Salespeople are born not made.
  - Salespeople must be good talkers.
  - Selling is knowing the right techniques and tricks.
  - A good salesperson can sell anything.

- There is no such creature as the 'all-rounder' that many companies are looking for. The 'all-rounder' only exists as an average. None of us is average. Your attributes are balanced by your disabilities. To become better at selling, focus on your attributes. In doing so, your disabilities will be crowded out.

- Knowledge, whilst important, can only ever be a foundation stone for a successful sales career. Customers assume you have knowledge about your product; you do not have to prove it by boring them to death.

In 1994, Dianne Summers[9] quoted research by the Kinnaird Communications Group, a Glasgow-based consultancy, claiming that:

---

[9]   Summers, D. (1994). 'Unloved and incompetent', *The Times*, 24 August.

... only 5% of field sales staff possess the requisite natural selling skills that make them stand out as professionals while 35% just manage to pay their way, leaving an astounding 60% just there for the beer.

Harsh criticism, indeed. Unfortunately, my own research shows a similar depressing picture.

Dave Lakhani[10] says that one of the most important characteristics a salesperson needs to have is adaptability. The mark of a truly exceptional salesperson is being able to take an eagle eye approach to the current situation and to develop a plan to leverage the industry, market, and company in one's favour for excelling and 'doing whatever it takes ... thinking differently, making extra calls, attaining laser-like focus, and being aggressive while still acting ethically is what this entails'.

Traits such as persuasiveness, determination, confidence, resilience, empathy, and ego drive, are all offered regularly as clues, together with the instruments to measure them. Graphology, psychology, topology, and kidology are sold by the real salespeople to those still searching for the natural born sales wonder. Like the emperor's clothes, the more often you say that there is a stereotype for the successful salesperson, the likelier it is to be true. Why is it then that all the successful salespeople I meet are different? Why am I constantly amazed by the diversity of successful salespeople? Why can I not find a 'norm' group? Could it be that one does not exist and that sales success has little to do with who you are but what you do?

Then there is the myth of 'closing technique' and the 153 ways of 'overcoming objections'. Why is it that in real life, during thousands of successful sales presentations, customers have no objections?

Each salesperson is unique, and true successful selling skills are to do with flexibility and adaptability to situations. For each sale, there is a different situation. But here is the conundrum. You can only adapt to the situation if you have something in your repertoire to use as the situation demands. Salespeople have been conned into

---

[10]   Lakhani, D. (2009). *How to Sell When Nobody's Buying (And How to Sell Even More When They Are)*, Hoboken, NJ: John Wiley & Sons, Inc.

believing that this preparation for different situations involves only learning to overcome objections and to close the sale.

I found, however, that these techniques only work in the classroom, mainly because the parties involved have a personal stake in maintaining the *status quo*. There is a game called 'You look after me and I'll look after you' – which means that, when we attend sales training courses, we do not make it too difficult for each other, as each will inevitably have to sell to the other in role-play. In addition, everyone agrees with the trainer on the day because life is easier that way. It makes little or no difference because whatever skills are learned on training courses are never implemented in the field anyway.

ATTRIBUTES OF A GOOD SALESPERSON

During a recent management training course, I asked the managers to help identify all the attributes that they believed should be possessed by a salesperson. I asked them to divide these attributes up into knowledge, skills, and attitude. They came up with the following list:

Knowledge

- **Company knowledge:** The company's history, reputation, and place in the market.
- **Industry knowledge:** Information about the wider market and which segment the company operates in and the competition.
- **Product knowledge:** Salespeople need to know all about the company's products and services, including the unique selling points (USPs) of the products, distinguishing between features and benefits.
- **Customer knowledge:** How the customer's business operates, with a basic financial understanding.

Skills

- **Sales skills:** Technique and ability.
- **Listening skills:** Analysing what people say and matching it to your products and services.

- **Interpersonal skills:** Showing the customer that you are interested in them.
- **Empathy:** Putting yourself in the customer's position.

Attitude

- Positive.
- Belief in own ability.
- Desire to improve.
- Desire to succeed.

They also came up with the following list that they found difficult to categorise:

Additional Attributes

- Confidence.
- Patience.
- Enthusiasm.
- Determination.
- Courage.
- Creativity.
- Conscientiousness.
- Honesty.
- Realism.
- Persistence.
- Assertive.
- Good humour.

In fact, it is easy to develop such a list, which appears to profile a being from another planet who is perfect in every respect: not requiring any training, able to manage their time effectively and needing little supervision, and prepared to work for next to nothing. In reality, such paragons do not exist.

SALESPEOPLE'S VIEWS

The problem does not just exist among those charged with managing salespeople. When I asked salespeople themselves "What makes a successful salesperson?", they came up with a similar list of attributes.

Interestingly, however, some contradictions emerged:

- 93% of salespeople I surveyed said they believed that customers buy from people they like. Yet 100% of the same salespeople said that 'like-ability' factors were less important than sales skills. In fact, empirical research places 'like-ability' very high on the buying motivation of consumers.

- 71% of salespeople agreed that practising selling skills regularly was important, yet 43% also felt that role-play was irrelevant.

- 21% felt there was no such thing as the 'natural-born sales wonder'. However, 86% also believed that, even given the same training, other salespeople were not as good as they were. What they were really saying was that there are no natural-born sales wonders apart from themselves. My experience has shown consistently that experienced salespeople, and especially sales managers, have the impression that everyone needs training apart from themselves.

- 80% said that sales training was imperative, yet 40% said they could have survived without any sales training at all.

- 99% did not choose selling as a first career choice. Much of this has to do with the image of selling and salespeople.

- 70% said that they would prefer to stay in a sales role, whilst the other 30% said that they had management aspirations. Having said that, less than 50% of salespeople had more than 8 years service with any one company.[11]

I also examined a number of demographic factors of salespeople, successful and unsuccessful. I discovered the following:

---

[11] Salisbury, F. (1989). 'Sales direction survey of sales management', *Sales Direction* /The Management Exchange.

- **Gender:** I found no evidence to support the theory that men are better salespeople than women or *vice versa.*
- **Experience:** Experience counts for nothing; experienced salespeople fail and succeed in equal numbers.
- **Successful track record:** Being successful in one company is no guarantee of being successful in a different company.
- **Age:** It does not matter how old or young you are; I meet successful and unsuccessful salespeople of all ages.

SALES PERSONALITY

As far back as 1965, Guion[12] said that not only do sales roles differ but also the personality characteristics required also vary greatly, and this is still true today. This whole area of personality and recruitment in sales is fraught with difficulties.

When I researched the field of using personality inventories to determine future sales success potential, I found the following flaws in their application and interpretation:

1. Personality researchers assume that people are predisposed to sales and that there exists an 'ideal' sales personality. From experience alone, you know people of widely different personalities in sales who are both successful and unsuccessful. Indeed, many unsuccessful salespeople join other companies and become successful, whilst successful salespeople leave to further their careers elsewhere only to become unsuccessful in their new position. In many of the sales forces I examined, I continually came across inconsistencies in personality amongst the top 20% of performers. In particular, most of the personality profiles would lead you to believe that successful salespeople are confident and goal orientated. My own findings showed that top salespeople are generally less confident internally and certainly more insecure than their lower performing colleagues. This is borne out by top performers in other fields. Insecurity appears to come with the

---

[12] Guion, R.M. (1965). *Personnel Testing,* Maidenhead: McGraw-Hill.

territory of high performance. Perhaps it is the uncertainty of not knowing how long this high performance level can last? Yet, when I attempted to apply this factor into a personality inventory, I found the same low correlations as exist in all other inventories. In addition, my own research clearly established that each company has its own 'personality'. In some cases, getting on with the boss's assistant and his/her favoured henchmen is a greater contributory factor to longevity of employment than a supposed sales personality. This leads me to the next point.

2. Hardly any company buying personality inventories conducts sufficient internal research in order to validate the instrument they are using. When I conducted my own research, I applied an instrument to a) all existing salespeople in the company, b) all applicants, and c) all new joiners over a 24-month period. I also attempted to keep in touch with applicants who were unsuccessful in their application. I drew up a profile of unsuccessful and successful internal salespeople and divided these between new starters and existing staff. I examined the profiles of applicants who were offered a job and those who were rejected. I monitored the sales results of all salespeople against these profiles over a two-year period. Last, I compared these results with demographic data to look for significant correlations. After two years, the profiles of successful and unsuccessful salespeople were close enough to be identical. I also examined in detail all of the inventories on the market and found the same low correlations. One of the biggest problems is that companies have no way of knowing whether the candidates they have rejected would have been successful.

3. All purveyors of personality inventories warn against using the results in isolation, stressing that they must be seen as part of a total process. In all cases where personality inventories were being used as part of a selection process, I observed a disproportionate credence being placed on the results of the inventory. Sales managers have a tendency to believe in instruments that are seen to be academically accredited, and that absolve them from making incorrect selection decisions. It should be said, however, that, in

processes where the only mechanism for deciding future potential is an interview, managers were generally wrong in 50% of cases. Even so, despite the guidance to avoid 'gut-feeling' on interviews, I found that 'gut-feeling' proved more intuitive at pre-guessing success than any inventory.

4. The greatest problem with personality inventories is that the candidates complete them themselves. I recall a quote from John Hillier (Chair of the National Council for Vocational Qualifications), who said, "I can convince myself that I am in control of my weight, provided I do not go anywhere near the scales". The tendency either to lie or to exaggerate is strong in salespeople wishing to make their biggest sale – employment. Most inventories contain a few questions that claim to be 'lie detectors'. Once again, I found that many salespeople know which these questions are and therefore learn to avoid making exaggerated claims about their ability in the questionnaire, only to save that exaggeration for the interview. Many managers, when interviewing, lack the skills to explore these exaggerated claims.

4. A question: If these inventories work, why have they not reduced labour turnover and failure, and increased success? They have not.

5. An observation: Some of the best salespeople I have ever met are those selling personality inventories!

Over the years, what I found was that successful salespeople contrasted with their less successful counterparts in that they:

- Displayed more energy.
- Showed more initiative in finding business.
- Displayed a confidence in their ability.
- Appeared to believe in what they were selling.
- Were fiercely loyal towards the company.
- Had a purpose in life and set clear goals with deadlines for achievement. But most importantly, and I have found this in all top performers in all professions, they accepted personal responsibility for their success *and* for any failures.

Nothing new you might say. Yet these could be described as behaviours – especially when coupled with the negative elements that emerged. I found that those who were failing were the type who:

- Instead of accepting responsibility for finding business, waited for the company to provide them with leads.
- Constantly made excuses about their performance, blaming it on the recession, the product, the weather or divine intervention.
- Hid from contact with the manager and their peer group.
- Displayed a negative attitude towards the company.
- Were devoid of goals or purpose.
- Failed to keep promises .
- Made exaggerated claims about their products.
- Exhibited superiority over the customer by using jargon.

You might hold the view that these salespeople were like this because of their failure, not that these behaviours caused their failure. The argument is irrelevant. Once in the trap, few rarely emerge. What you have here though are two sets of behaviours, which can be used to create a greater level of self-awareness regarding your own behaviour.

In addition, I found that successful salespeople had more:

- Self-knowledge.
- Knowledge of product benefits.
- Knowledge of internal contacts who could help them.
- Desire to be in selling.
- Respect for the customer.

An important factor, which separates top-performing salespeople from the rest, is in their attitude towards the customer. They know that they will continue to be successful only by helping other people get what they want. Successful salespeople are customer-focussed rather than sales-focussed; they employ low pressure sales processes rather than high pressure selling techniques; they understand the difference between 'I win and you win' and 'I win and you lose'; and they would rather say the customer bought than was sold to.

WHAT MAKES A GOOD SALESPERSON DISTINCTIVE?

Tom Hopkins[13] produced a profile of the successful salesperson, from which you usually can identify them from the moment they walk into the room. A good salesperson:

- **Takes great pride in their appearance, and this attitude radiates to the customer:** They believe that they are in the presence of someone important; hence they take that person very seriously.

- **Is confident, but not overconfident:** They are confident because they know that they are equipped with all the knowledge necessary to help their customers reach an informed decision about the products they are trying to sell.

- **Is capable of motivating themselves to do well:** They have belief in themselves and their abilities to succeed.

- **Want to achieve:** Furthermore, they have an intense passion that drives them to achieve and keep on achieving.

- **Does not shy away from confronting his/her own personal demons:** They will always strive to conquer the aspects of their job that they find intimidating, and subsequently learn from these experiences.

- **Is still positive, even if they fail:** They do not let an individual failure affect their future performances. Instead, they take stock of what has happened and build a learning experience from it so that they can excel in the future.

- **Have a firm belief in the process of on-going training:** They are aware of the fact that they can never know too much about their job; hence they are willing to move forward and embrace new ideas. Furthermore, they are not reluctant to learn.

---

[13] Hopkins, T (1983). *How To Master the Art of Selling*, London: Grafton Books.

KNOWLEDGE

Knowledge, it is said, forms the basis of a salesperson's career. Without knowledge of the company's products, the market available, and the role of the company in that market, a salesperson may be placed at a disadvantage by customers' questions about the product, a situation that ultimately could result in missed sales opportunities.

Some managers and trainers advocate product competency in salespeople – but a word of warning. Many salespeople know everything there is to know about their company's products, have a total appreciation of where the market is and a clear understanding of their company's place in that market, but they could not sell water to a thirsty man. Every sales force has experts who cannot sell.

Yet, whenever you ask salespeople what they would like more training in, if any, product knowledge always comes top of the list. Over a seven-year period, I conducted a number of surveys about the training and development needs of salespeople. Top of the list each time came the need for more product knowledge training – at least, the perceived need for product knowledge. There is a theory that the need for product knowledge courses increases in direct proportion to the number of product knowledge courses available.

Product knowledge training provides a safe haven for poor salespeople. In my experience, there is rarely a need for product knowledge training in a company after initial training, unless a new product is being launched and, even then, it is doubtful how much is necessary. Anyone can acquire product knowledge. If salespeople were tested before running a course, most companies probably would be surprised by how much they already know. In fact, if periodic testing were made compulsory, and employment depended on having it, companies would be amazed how competent their salespeople would become!

SALES SKILLS

Of far more use to salespeople than knowledge is a concentration on learning sales skills. The danger is that too many people believe that skills are acquired on a training course. All a training course can ever do is to make you aware of the need to learn a skill. The acquisition of a skill takes considerably longer than any company can afford to allow you to stay in a classroom. One way to understand this process is by referring to **Figure 3**.

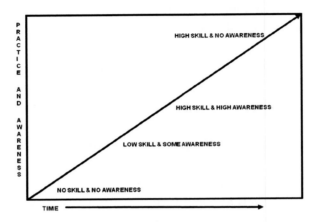

Figure 3: Skills Acquisition

Think of the time before you learned how to drive a car. You were at the bottom left of the model: 'no skill, no awareness'. Sitting next to someone else who is skilled at driving is deceptive. It looks easy, because they make it look easy. You could be forgiven for saying to yourself, "I could do that. It looks simple enough, and anyway, if they can do it I'm sure I could too". The same is true of a sport such as snooker. It looks easy enough on television. When you first try and play it, however, you realise almost immediately how difficult it is. The next step in the model is where you move to some awareness of your low skill. You try driving for the first time. For most of us, we were told how to start the car. Most of us completely ignored the instruction and either stalled the car or nearly burnt out the starter motor in our keenness to show our level of competence, which at this stage is non-existent.

Driving is a skill that cannot be learned from discussion, from books or watching someone else do it. It is something you have to experience, something you have to do. It is a physical skill.

Playing snooker is a skill that cannot be learned from discussion, books or watching someone else do it. It is something you have to experience, something you have to 'do'. It is a physical skill.

Athletics, acting, music, dancing are all skills based. You cannot learn these things from discussion, books or watching someone else do them. They are activities you have to experience, something you have to do. They are physical skills.

Selling is a skill. It cannot be learned from discussion, books or watching someone else do it. It is something you have to experience, something you have to 'do'. It is a physical skill. That is why so many salespeople are at the bottom of this model. It is only through practising the skill that we can become aware of the potential length of the journey. Practice and failure makes us aware of where we are – like learning to drive. Only when you first get behind the wheel of the car do you realise how much there is to learn. The same principle should apply to selling. Yet, in most cases, salespeople, sales managers, and sales trainers fail to understand the analogy.

In selling, we use physical skills: speech, tone, words, eye movements, facial expressions, and body movements. We can use touch (handshakes and pats, etc). But because these are learned at such an early age, we forget the process we went through to acquire the skill of communication. In this way, there comes a time when we stop learning. By practising a skill, we move up the model to the level of high skill and high awareness. We do things in a deliberate way to bring about a physical performance. We know how to do it, but it has not become innate enough yet to stop thinking about it all the time we are doing it. Think about your driving test. You exhibit a level of high skill, sufficient to pass your test, yet it can be and usually is tiring. Carrying out a physical task and thinking about all of the movements associated with that task is hard work. It can be exhausting. Depress the clutch at the same time as easing off the accelerator. Check the mirror while keeping an eye on your speed. Switch the indicator on whilst looking at your wing mirror and the traffic ahead.

We fail to realise just how much is involved because, as we become competent in a particular task or skill, it becomes innate and we do not have to think about it anymore. This process continues until such time as we reach the top of the model: high skill, no awareness. The skill becomes innate. We do it without having to think about it. We drive to work without remembering the journey; it has become an automatic function. Some days, when we are supposed to go somewhere else, we find ourselves on the same route to work. Is it dangerous? No. We are quite safe. The actual skill of driving has become so innate that we do not have to even think about it. When something happens out of the ordinary, we can react in time to deal with it. However, it can be quite disconcerting on a long journey to realise suddenly "I can't remember the last few exits on the motorway!"

The same process applies to selling. We can become highly skilled at the physical parts of the process so that we forget that we are standing still in skills terms. The problem is that there are no easy answers to successful selling, just hard work, and for some reason we have found salespeople not to understand the relationship between hard work and success. Perhaps that is being less than generous, as many salespeople will say "I do work hard – it's just that it isn't happening for me at the moment". My response is usually "Working hard at what?" There are of course psychological issues to consider about practice and working hard: **Figure 4** explains what I mean.

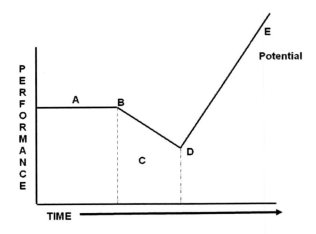

Figure 4: Performance over Time

Over a period of time, we tend to settle at a level of performance that we feel comfortable with (point A). This level could be high, low, or average, but the fact is that we have great difficulty in moving that performance significantly without some form of intervention by someone else, be that a manager, a trainer, or a colleague. For many salespeople, it usually involves moving to another company and starting off fresh, where the grass is inevitably greener. I see nothing wrong with salespeople moving around (and most salespeople up to the age of 40 do so every three or four years). However, I also believe that many could be as successful as their aspirations in their present company, if only they practised their sales skills more often.

The difficulty arises when that practice begins. If we have been performing at a particular level (A) for some considerable time, then a training event (at point B) is more likely to have an adverse effect on our performance, than if practice was a normal function of our jobs. Trying to improve someone's skills requires change and, as we know, change is not comfortable at any time, never mind change that involves learning to do something differently.

The reason for this is that learning to enhance your performance or learning to do things differently requires a significant amount of practice. During this period, it is quite common for performance levels to drop (point D). If you play golf, you may understand the principle. Most amateur golfers play off a certain handicap score for years without seeing any dramatic movement in their handicap figure. Once in a while they might be motivated to take a lesson from the golf club professional. Inevitably, the coaching results in the golfer having to change a particular facet of their play: stand differently, or hold their club differently, or alter the height of their swing. Whatever it is, both during practise and eventual play, the golfer experiences a drop in performance. When this happens to a professional golfer, they continue with the practice until such time as the new or enhanced skill is mastered, eventually realising a higher overall performance level (point E). The critical period for amateurs and, we have to say, for many salespeople is at point C – the danger zone. It is where things are not going well and they give up, returning to their previous performance level (A). This is where you hear many salespeople and amateurs say, "I tried that once and it didn't work". I know of no other profession where people say, "I tried that once and it didn't work". You must make up your own mind whether to stay an amateur or become a professional. For all of us, learning involves a process of improvement, setbacks and plateauing. Professionals understand this, amateurs are fazed by it.

In 1990, when I had completed our initial research into selling, sales processes and salespeople, I found that many salespeople fell into two distinct categories (**Figure 5**):

- The competent technician who was also a sales disaster.

- The sales genius who was also the technical incompetent.

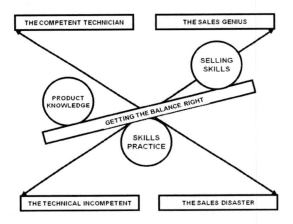

Figure 5: Getting the Balance Right

There is no one thing that makes a good salesperson. It is a combination of knowledge, skill and attitude. Each is important and necessary, but the combinations may vary. In a hierarchy of sales success, however, knowledge should only ever be the foundation stone of success – vital but not enough on its own. It is the application of that knowledge or skill that is vital – but what dictates success more than anything else is your attitude.

ATTITUDE

Let us suppose that the job you do has been identified as requiring the following skills:

- Listening.
- Questioning.
- Presenting.

Is listening a skill or an attitude? Do people have poor listening skills because of a lack of training, or a lack of interest? Is listening a matter of poor attitude, or poor hearing? Are people bad at asking questions because they do not know how, or do they lack the motivation to find out about other people? Is presenting simply a matter of acquiring the skill to do so? What about people who are terrified of making presentations to groups of people (most of us are like this)? Is the manner in which people communicate a matter of training, or of conditioning, and if the latter is true, can that be defined as being part of our personality make-up or attitude? What is skill? Is it an innate ability that you are born with? Can anybody acquire any sort of skill? If most skills can be identified as being substantially influenced by attitude, can they be changed or enhanced?

Most selling skills are attitudinally based. It is certain that, barring physical disability, we all already can perform most of the skills that we are asked to perform in a sales role. That is to say, we can physically perform those skills, given time, practice, and feedback. So what stops us? When I asked a number of sales managers this question about their salespeople, they came up with the following reasons:

- Wrong person for the job.
- Bad attitude.
- Not motivated.
- Useless.
- I did not pick them.

The last response is known as the 'inheritance factor'. Notice that 'attitude' appears again. So if it is all about attitude, what can you do about it? Some people say that you cannot change attitude, but I believe you can. Festinger[14] showed that, by changing behaviour, attitude changes also were possible. Obviously it takes a long time, but then so does learning any new skill or changing firmly-held beliefs. Festinger said that, by changing behaviour, a cognitive dissonance is created, which is only relieved by changing attitudes to suit the new behaviour. People are not born with an attitude, they acquire one through beliefs and feelings and experiences throughout their lives and, in this way, attitude can be a dynamic entity. As we get older, however, we take on board fewer attitude-changing beliefs, as we harden ourselves to the pain of change.

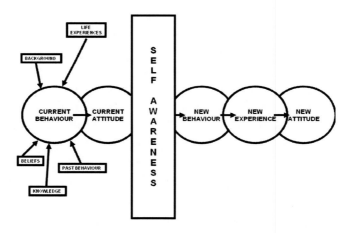

Figure 6: How Behaviour Shapes Attitude

Our background, our life experiences, the past behaviours we see and adopt, together with the knowledge and beliefs we collect, determine our current behaviour and hence our current attitude. Our attitude is changed by an increasing self-awareness, which produces a new behaviour, leads to new experiences, and develops into a new attitude. There is the story about Mark Twain, who was reported to have said that, when he was 16, he was dismayed by his father,

---

14 Festinger, L. (1964). 'Behavioural support for opinion change', *Public Opinion Quarterly*, Vol. 28.

whom he reasoned to be probably the stupidest man in the world. Years later, he said, "By the time I became 21, I was amazed how much my father had learned".

A good example of changed behaviour leading to changed attitude is those people who say, "When we have children, we are determined that it will not change our lives". Those of us who have children know how wrong that premise, and that attitude, is. Whether we like it or not, or try and resist it or not, the effect of having children, watching them grow, and being responsible for them, makes an enormous difference to our lives. With hindsight, we would not say, "It won't change our lives". The fact is that the adoption of new behaviours gives us new values, feelings, and attitudes.

However, most people are not very good at 'navel-gazing'. Sometimes, what we see in ourselves is not what others see. For a start, our image in the mirror is exactly that – a mirror image. If you want to know what you look like to other people, scan a photograph of yourself into a graphics programme that will allow you to reverse the image. It is quite disconcerting to see this for the first time!

Our behaviour changes when we get to know people better, especially after we have spent time together. It is a fact that the more time people spend together, the more they get to like each other. Like so many myths, familiarity does not breed contempt, but liking. However, our attitude towards meeting new people rarely changes, simply because the behaviour that precedes it usually follows a pattern that includes some of the following:

- Looking tentatively for a face we recognise.
- Appearing apprehensive.
- Scanning the room for someone who looks in charge so that we can introduce ourselves.
- Not sitting down until we work out where we should sit or are expected to sit.
- Not introducing ourselves until we have established eye contact.

To an outsider, we look less than confident and, as we do not get any feedback on that behaviour, we repeat it.

SELF-AWARENESS

Acquiring self-awareness is not easy. Lasting change, and the self-awareness that sparks it, requires help. The most obvious source of this help is your coach. The coach, by helping you become more aware, by encouraging new behaviours, can provide the spur to help you gain the sort of attitude that winners need.

Defining the right attitude is a complex issue. I hear a lot about having a positive mental attitude in sales and I would go along with the theory that positive people tend to be more successful at selling than negative people. It does, however, remain a theory. I have met plenty of miserable salespeople who appear to be successful, but I do believe that attitude counts more than either knowledge or skills in isolation. A person with the right attitude can succeed in any case, but having both knowledge and skills rarely works without the right attitude. However, attitude sometimes has been confused with behaviour and displaying a positive attitude perhaps could be just as effective as actually possessing one.

Whilst most organisations I have dealt with agree that a positive attitude is an essential attribute of successful salespeople, most struggle with finding any way to improve it in their salespeople. The school of thought expressed by Chrissy[15] says that behavioural training should be a requisite for all salespeople. On the other hand, Rae[16] says that you cannot hope to change people's behaviour – the best you can do is to make people more aware of the effect their behaviour has on other people.

Perhaps salespeople need the sort of attitude that makes them want to learn more about their current attitudes and the way in which their behaviour affects others. Unfortunately, this desire to open the Pandora's Box rarely exists. Whilst I have found salespeople to be narcissistic and interested in examining their personality characteristics, they soon become sceptical when adverse feedback is

---

[15] Chrissy, W.J.E. (1969). Salesmanship: *The Personal Force in Marketing*, Hoboken, NJ: John Wiley & Sons Ltd.

[16] Rae, L. (1985): *The Skills of Human Relations Training*, London: Gower.

given, and seldom want to examine or have others observe their negative behaviour.

So, let us suppose that a salesperson is identified as having a negative attitude. How can this be changed to a positive attitude? That is the £1m question to which all companies are seeking the answer. On the one hand, I know that, through perseverance, a coach or a manger can force behavioural change that, in theory, will bring about attitudinal change but most managers find it difficult to gauge whether an individual salesperson has accepted the need for attitudinal change or is merely feigning acceptance. Change of attitude can take an inordinate amount of time. It becomes even more difficult if it is something you attempt to do yourself without professional help. I do not mean help from a psychoanalyst but rather from a professional coach.

A coach can help those who want to change and improve to do so and this leads me to the final point: you have to want to. Not just want to improve but want to change. Everyone would like to improve their performance, but change is a less of a desirable goal for most people. Yet, your current behaviour delivers your current results. Therefore, in order to change your results for the better, you have to change your behaviour. This does not happen on training courses; it happens after the training course.

I know from experience that people can be motivated on courses to accept that an improvement in their attitude by changing their behaviour will improve their results. I am also enough in touch with reality to accept that this motivation is cursory and lasts only as long as nothing happens to break the spell after the training event – such as breathing! The motivation to change might last for a day, or an hour. However, that hour may just be enough to make someone want to do something about changing instead of just thinking about doing something. For it to work, you have to already have decided that it is time you did something different. As Vincent T. Lombardi says: "The difference between a successful person and others is not a lack of strength, not a lack of knowledge, but rather a lack of will".

NEXT ...

- In your opinion, what makes a good salesperson?
- How important is personality in professions such as sports or the performing arts, and what can you learn from this with regard to selling – or is selling a completely different issue?
- When was the last time you attended a sales training course that contained an element of sales skills improvement? What happened after the training event? Have you returned to the way you used to sell or have you altered your skill base? What might you learn from this?

CHAPTER 4

PROCESS

SUMMARY

- There is no evidence to support the existence of an effective off-the-shelf structured sales process, although many writers advocate a number of desirable approaches.

- In a similar vein, the process of closing sales and of overcoming objections receives both positive support and negative commentary.

- You should explore these subjects in greater depth by analysing the success (or otherwise) of your use of these techniques.

- A tighter structure to the sales presentation can have a beneficial effect on controlling the sales interview.

MODELS OF SELLING

Many salespeople, trainers and managers, advocate that having a systematic structure to a sales presentation works, and in some cases, is a prerequisite to sales success. As far back as 1971, Robertson's[17] research suggested that the models that appeared most often in sales literature were Palda's Hierarchical Effects Model,[18] Tosdal's AIDA Model,[19] and Nakanishi's Adoption Process Model[20] (**Figure 7**).

---

[17] Robertson, T. (1971). *Innovative Behaviour and Communication*, Geneva, IL: Holt & Rinehart.

[18] Palda, K.S. (1966). 'The hypothesis of a hierarchy of effects', *Journal of Marketing*, Vol. 63, January.

[19] Tosdal, H.R. (1925). *Principles of Personal Selling*, New York: McGraw-Hill.

Models of Selling

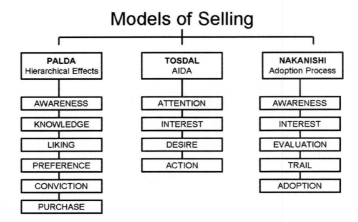

Figure 7: Models of Selling

Since then there have been, and continues to be, a plethora of sales models created such as SPIN,[21] Strategic Selling™,[22] and innumerable Seven Step Selling models. The most widely recognised and taught on many courses over the years has been AIDA (Attention, Interest, Desire, and Action). Yet even this model, it was suggested by Eugene Johnson,[23] was derived from an even earlier system advocated by Arthur Frederick Sheldon[24] in 1916 called AIDR, which stood for Attention, Interest, Desire, and Resolve. There are, in fact, a variety of models based on AIDA and the originality of it is somewhat lost in the mists of time. Some even say that AIDA was developed by St.

[20] Nakanishi, M. (1971). *Consumer Learning in Awareness and Trial of New Products*, Duluth, MN: Association for Consumer Research.

[21] Rackham, N. (1988). *SPIN Selling*, New York: McGraw-Hill. (SPIN stands for Situation, Problem, Implication, Need.)

[22] Miller, R.B., Heiman, S.E. and Tuleja, T. (1988). *Strategic Selling: The Unique Sales System Proven by America's Best Companies*, New York: Grand Central Publishing.

[23] Johnson, E.M. *et al.* (1986). *Sales Management Concepts, Practices, and Cases*, New York: McGraw-Hill.

[24] Arthur Frederick Sheldon (1868-1935) was the founder of the Sheldon School for the Teaching of Business Science, which opened in 1902. In 1915, at the height of his school's popularity, over 10,000 students from around the world were enrolled.

Elmo Lewis[25] in the 19th century. Selling truly has been with us for a long time.

All in all, the theory of AIDA is grab the customer's attention, find out what they are interested in, stimulate their desire to buy your product, and close in on the sale – which, in reality, is not far short of the mark.

What I found is that, whilst most generic sales structures work well enough on sales training courses, when peer pressure makes you believe in a particular system, in front of a customer the vast majority fall far short of being of any practical use. Training organisations sell sales structures, not because they work, but because they are easy to sell to salespeople and sales trainers. We are all looking for the easy answer to sales success.

Although their ineffectiveness suggests their impact on quality is minimal, unfortunately some teach people selling techniques that leave a customer feeling they have been interrogated. Interrogation is not a desirable feature of a quality relationship.

My own research showed that over 60% of salespeople and sales managers feel that adopting a structured approach to selling should work, and is desirable, and yet the same people said they found it difficult to put into practice. Sales managers I questioned about what actually happened in the field said they saw little evidence of any structure being used by the vast majority of salespeople, and certainly not by those salespeople who were successful.

There is no empirical evidence to support the practice of teaching salespeople a sales structure. There is, however, evidence that shows the practice of closing techniques is detrimental to the sales process, rather than helpful. Neil Rackham's research[26] (probably the largest research project on selling ever undertaken in the UK) has shown repeatedly that manipulative closing techniques are a myth. In fact, his work suggests that such techniques only work for low cost

---

[25] St. Elmo Lewis (1872-1948) was an American advertising guru who wrote and spoke about the potential of advertising to educate the public. He was the co-founder/first president of the Association of National Advertisers and was inducted into the Advertising Hall of Fame three years after his death.

[26] Rackham, N. (1987). *Making Major Sales,* London: Gower.

unimportant purchases. They are more likely to have a negative impact on serious buying decisions. Nobody should find this surprising, for how do you react to aggressive pushy salespeople? Are you more likely to buy a product you clearly object to? The techniques for responding to such objections are often manipulative, with the assumption that people are not capable of thinking logically. Rackham again shows that the more objections that are raised during a meeting, the less likely a sale will be made. His work also shows that the more experienced and successful the salesperson, the fewer objections he or she will encounter.

There is a strong school of thought that says that selling has more to do with personal relationships and behaviour than learning a technique. Whilst it is difficult to disagree with this, it is however a far more difficult and time-consuming approach to learn. For this reason, many trainers go for the easy process of structured selling and closing techniques.

Your greatest challenge is to decide which behaviours you want to learn. Listening to many successful salespeople, I was able to feel the difference, but putting it into words proved perplexing. It seems that successful salespeople act naturally, and indeed I know a significant number of successful salespeople whose only common trait is that they are being themselves.

Robinson[27] said that salespeople are not very good at acting naturally, and that the main purpose of role play is to help salespeople identify their natural traits, and to use them to full advantage. My own findings reinforce this view, and that leads me to the problem of time and expense. The problem for organisations and trainees alike is that this form of adaptive (or insight response) training is expensive. The single most cost-effective way of carrying this out, however, is by field coaching.

The debate about behaviour, and whether it can be changed or not, goes on. Perhaps the best that can be expected is a greater understanding of the effect that your behaviour has on other people.

---

[27] Robinson, L.B. (1987). 'Role-playing as a sales training tool', *Harvard Business Review*, May/June.

Again, self-awareness can lead to improvement in behaviour. If you know that a particular set of behaviours is contributing to difficulty in sales relationships, then you would be silly to continue displaying those behaviours.

It is possible to change behaviour, given time and professional assistance. There are however no easy answers. Weitz[28] believes that this is because there are no universally effective sales behaviours. He said that all sales jobs are different, and even each sales situation is different. Mistakenly in my view, because of this, too many salespeople and trainers believe that you have to be totally flexible in your approach.

A SIMPLE HIGH LEVEL STRUCTURE

In simple terms, I have found that top salespeople:

- Sell themselves and their companies first.
- Find out what customers want by asking relevant questions.
- Match their products and services to the customer's wants and needs.
- Are not frightened to ask for the order, but do so by presenting all the previous agreements in a logical final buying agreement.

Figure 8 presents this sales process.

---

[28] Weitz, B.A. (1979). *A Critical Review of Personal Selling Research*, Eugene, OR: University of Oregon.

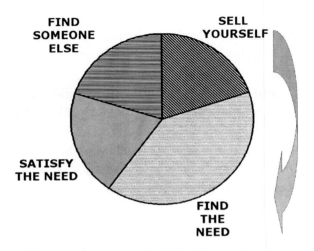

Figure 8: The Sales Process

Sell yourself
The most important part of any sales call is the opening or introduction. There should be agreement between you and the customer on why you wanted to talk to them, and how you intend to conduct the discussion. It also is useful to include at the beginning of the discussion, "If you find this product useful, I'd like to think that you would refer me to a colleague or someone else you know who would also benefit from it".

Find the need
By asking the customer questions, it is up to you to find out as much about the customer's needs and wants as you can. In addition, it is important to check with the customer that your understanding matches theirs.

Satisfy the need
This is about matching your product solutions to the customer's needs and wants, for example: "If I was able to provide you with this product, would it satisfy the need you have?" Importantly, if they say "No", find out why. Too many salespeople give up just because the customer said "No". Quite often it can be due to some misunderstanding that can be cleared easily: "So what you're saying is that if the product did that, you would be willing to try it?" Then

you should review everything again just to make absolutely certain that there is no misunderstanding.

Find someone else

The best sources of future prospects are your current customers. You should ask on each call, whether the call has been successful or not, for a referred lead – for example, "As I said at the beginning, ... etc".

A STRUCTURED PROCESS FOR SECOND CALLS

If the product or service you are selling involves a two-call sales process, such as selling life assurance, then I recommend the following four-stage process:

- Your last agreement.
- The tangible benefits.
- The personal intangible benefits.
- Your recommendations.

Your last agreement

Whenever there is a break in the sales process, whether it is for a minute or a week, it is important to recreate the last positive buying atmosphere before you start selling again. Clearly, if you are on the second call, the chances are that you have created enough of a positive atmosphere; otherwise you would not have been invited back. The first thing to do, therefore, is to re-affirm the agreement reached last time – for example, "Just to go back over where we got to last time. You said that you were interested in the XYZ model, and you asked me to bring a quotation with me that included ABC. That's right, isn't it?"

The tangible benefits

Each product or service normally has at least one tangible and one intangible benefit – for example, the tangible benefit of an alarm system is that it makes a noise if someone breaks in. So you would say, "You saw how much noise this alarm would make. It's enough to wake the dead. We also fit it near the gable end of the house, ensuring that it can't be tampered with easily. And, as I mentioned last time, it is rust-proof. Last, your insurance company will give you a 5% discount on your home insurance if you install it".

Before going any further, you must check that the customer is still satisfied with these benefits before proceeding – for example, "So just before I go on, are you are still happy that these items suit your current needs?" If the customer brings something else up, or disagrees with a particular point, then it is back to the drawing board!

The personal intangible benefits

If the customer is happy with the last stage, you then seek agreement again on the intangible benefits – for example, "You felt when we talked before that this would give you further peace of mind, and that it would be good to see the cost of your insurance coming down instead of going up. Are you still happy with these benefits?"

Your recommendations

It should then be a straightforward matter of tying all the parts of your presentation together – for example, "Well, what I have managed to do is to produce a quote within the costs you said you would be comfortable with, for the XYZ model, which also includes ABC. It satisfies the requirements you had for (tangible benefits) as well as (intangible benefits), and if you are happy to go ahead on that basis, all I need is for you to OK this confirmation order".

Does it work?

The last question in the 'Who wants to be a sales training millionaire' quiz is "Does having a structured sales process work?" The answer is "Yes" and "No". Although the empirical evidence is not published, and therefore not open to scrutiny, I know from my own experience that having a structure works. But it does depend on what type of structure you employ and herein lies the rub. I might be able to convince you that the above four-part structure is the key to sales success – but what does it actually mean and how do you use it? In reality, as it is with the vast majority of sales models on offer, it is so vague as to be open to a wide variety of interpretations. Some sellers of similar models also may convince you that the vagueness belies its strength in that your task is to use the model as a framework, and then fill in the detail based on your own market, product, and service, and I do not have a problem with that. Other than making it absolutely clear that a framework is all that it is. It is not complicated and hardly a secret – but then this may lie at the heart of effective selling.

What I would say is that structure is important. It is important because it allows you to prepare and adapt as appropriate, based on the specific product you sell, and the specific needs of a specific customer. But if the structure is too vague, is there a more detailed structure? The answer is "Yes". And it is either being used by someone in the company or it is still to be developed, tested, refined and implemented by you.

A SYSTEMATIC SALES PROCESS

In **Chapter 2**, I presented the Professional Process Model (**Figure 2**), the core elements of which included a consistent and inflexible application of rules, basic training, and use of tools. I now present this as more of a business-related model shown in **Figure 9**.

Figure 9: The Professional Processes Model adapted

Surprisingly, whilst most companies have processes and procedures for elements of their operations such as finance, quality control, compliance, and even ordering stationery, what happens face-to-face with the customer is rarely written down. Having a clearly-defined sales process is fundamental to adopting a professional approach to the sales function and the contents of a well-defined sales process do not just include the customer transaction. Additionally, it should include what happens before and after contact and communication with a customer.

In **Figure 10**, you can see a template for a standard sales process that covers most, if not all, elements of a sales process no matter what specific job or industry you operate in.

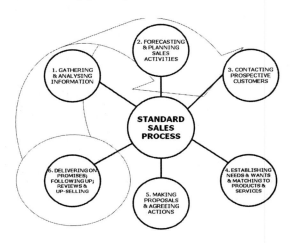

Figure 10: The Sales Process Template

Gathering and analysing information

The questions you need to ask yourself at this stage include:

- What is the source of your existing customer information and where is this held?

- How do you analyse this information in terms of deciding where the potential for further and cross-sales might exist?

- Where is the source of information about prospective customers and how is this accessed/available?

- How do you analyse this information in terms of deciding where the potential for future sales might exist (qualifying prospects)?

- What do you know about your competitors and which existing and potential customers might be buying from them, and why?

- What is unique about your product and services and what is unique about your competitor's products and services?
- How much time in an average week do you spend on gathering and analysing customer and prospect information?
- What could be improved in this aspect of your job?

The purpose of asking yourself these questions is to stimulate your thought processes to determine whether the effort you are expending here is worth it – "Am I spending the right amount of time seeing the right people?" This will be true of each of the elements of the standard sales process below.

Forecasting and planning sales activities
There's another adage, very true of selling: 'It's not that people plan to fail, they fail to plan'. Some of the questions applicable here include:

- How are your sales plans for the year/quarter/month/week/day put together?
- How do you plan your time in any one day/week/month?
- What systems/tools do you use to allocate your time?
- How do you know whether the activity you are engaged in will achieve your target?
- Who is involved in planning and forecasting with you?
- How much time do you allocate each day/week to planning and forecasting?
- How do you monitor progress?
- What records are maintained regarding this activity?
- What improvements could be made to this part of your job?

Contacting prospective and existing customers
Questions here include:

- How do you make contact with prospective customers?
- What works best? Is there a best time/method?
- How much time do you spend each day/week/month contacting customers?

- If you telephone prospective customers what do you say? What is the response?
- How are referrals handled? How successful is this? How many might you get in a week/month?
- How often do you get introductions from other colleagues? What happens? Can you give examples? Why does it not happen more?
- How often do you introduce your customers to other colleagues? Can you give examples? What stops you from doing it more often?
- How could this area of your work be improved?

Establishing needs and wants and matching these to products and services

The recommended methodology is always to test out solutions before proposing them. Questions here include:

- How do you establish what it is the customer is looking for? How do you usually begin?
- Is there a system you use? Is there a format? Is there a fact-find? How do you record the discussion?
- How do you know that the way in which you do this works?
- What are you trying to sell to the customer?
- How easy/difficult is it to expand the conversation outside of what the customer might be specifically looking for to the rest of your product/service range?
- How do you handle the competition when it comes up in conversation?
- Think about a time when the discussion went well. What happened? What did you learn?
- Think about a time when the discussion did not go well. What happened? What did you learn?
- What feedback do you get about your customer interviews? How often are you observed?
- How could this area of your work be improved?

Making proposals and agreeing actions

Some people call this closing. If the first few elements of the process are done correctly, there is no need to close. The customer simply ends up buying. Questions here include:

- How do you close the business?
- Is there a formal process to agreeing action?
- Do you have any idea of your strike rate (the number of successful interviews over number of interviews)?
- How many people might you meet and interview in a typical day/week/month?
- How many meetings does it normally take to close the business?
- What is stopping you from doing more customer interviews?
- What stops customers from making decisions?
- Think about a time when this area of your job went really well. What happened? What did you learn?
- Think about a time when this area of your job did not go well. What happened? What did you learn?
- How could this area of your job be improved?

Delivering on promises, following up, reviewing, and up-selling

Questions here include:

- What happens after the sale?
- How do you ensure that the agreements reached with the customer actually happen?
- How do you up-sell?
- How often do you ask for a referral? What do you say? How often is this successful?
- What happens if you did not get the sale?
- What records do you keep?
- What feedback do you get about your performance overall and specifically?
- Think about a time when something went really well with regard to referrals. What happened? What did you learn?

- Think about a time when something did not go well with regard to referrals. What happened? What did you learn?
- How could this area of your job be improved?

Using this approach, the sales process is unique to you. It becomes your game plan.

The benefit of having your game plan written down is that it becomes your blueprint for how to sell. It can be regularly updated in order to cope with changes such as:

- New products and services.
- New markets.
- New entry competition.

Sometimes there is more than one process, each one applicable to a certain market or type of customer.

NEXT ...

- What are the advantages and disadvantages to having a sales structure?
- When you have been aware of someone using closing techniques on you what was the outcome? What have you deduced from this?
- If you have ever attended a training event where these methods of overcoming objections were taught, what has been your experience of using them with the customer? What have you deduced from this?

CHAPTER 5
PROSPECTING

SUMMARY

- High achievers never stop prospecting.
- Leave letter writing to the experts. It is a function of marketing rather than selling. Letters are only useful to salespeople as a pre-approach means of providing confidence before making a telephone call.
- There is nothing wrong with cold-calling in order to make appointments – you might run the risk of achieving some business!
- Email still has a very low success strike rate.
- The jury is still out on the effectiveness of social media as a means of gaining customers, with anecdotal evidence being both positive and negative.

Most salespeople refer to identifying buyers as 'prospecting', and to potential customers as 'prospects'. Prospecting is the easiest topic to teach, but the most difficult thing to motivate yourself to do, which does not stop companies from saying "If we knew how to get in front of prospects, we wouldn't need to employ salespeople in the first place!" New sales recruits often are heard to say, "They show you how to overcome objections, how to close, how to sell yourself, but then these things are not difficult anyway. The difficult part is finding enough people to sell to, and they never show you that".

You probably already know that your level of business is never constant. It can grow or diminish in volume, depending on a great many factors. The danger with being busy is that sometimes you can reduce looking for new business, which ultimately affects revenue. Some of the reasons why sales can decline include:

- Customers retire or go out of business because of ill health, death, and financial difficulties or for personal reasons.
- Customers may stop doing business with your company.
- Customers may merge or be taken over by another company.
- Customers may relocate outside of your area.
- Your contact may be promoted or leave.

You should consider prospecting as being the foundation of your sales career – for salespeople, it is a truism that 'without prospects, you have no prospects'. Over the years, however, it is in this area of a salesperson's work that I have seen the greatest level of failure. It is not that the world is devoid of prospects, it is just that prospecting is seen by many salespeople as a depressing activity because of the inherent potential personal rejection element.

SOCIAL MEDIA

As the 21st century unfolds, many salespeople hope that the expanding use of the internet and mobile communication somehow will solve some of the problems and stress associated with prospecting. This is especially so in younger salespeople, though not exclusively, who seek to expand their circle of contacts through social media,[29] such as Facebook, YouTube, LinkedIn and Twitter. Although the numbers of people attracted to these social media sites and like methods of communicating are staggering, the jury is still out on their effectiveness, and there can be dangers associated with the speed of any negative publicity, if it happens, reaching a large audience.

Yet these social media sites are no more than a technological extension of older-style networking methods, such as actually attending meetings and social events – though networking *via* the web saves time and effort. I eventually gave up attending a local Business Breakfast Club, which met once a month and whose

---

[29]   http://www.youtube.com/watch?v=sIFYPQjYhv8&feature=player_detailpage

intention was to bring the local business community together and encourage the prospect of business introductions and hence sales. The problem was that, over a period of two years, the only people I increasingly seemed to meet were life coaches – most of whom did not appear to have lived very much, and none of whom were potential customers.

UNQUALIFIED AND QUALIFIED PROSPECTS

Unqualified prospects are those who possibly might buy your product or services and whom you have not yet placed in the qualified prospect category. Qualified prospects are people or organisations that you have established either want or need your product, may qualify financially to purchase, and insofar as the individual is concerned, have the authority to influence or make the ultimate buying decision. Customers are people who are buying from you or have bought in the past (**Figure 11**).

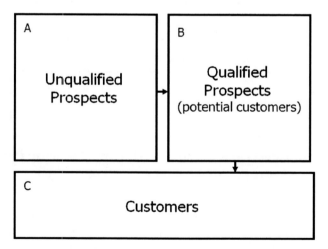

Figure 11: Prospects and Customers I

In drawing up your initial prospecting list, everyone could be called an unqualified prospect. Yet all unqualified prospects will not necessarily become qualified prospects, or be categorised as potential customers.

If you do nothing but look after your current customers, then the size of that customer base might diminish over time. This is especially relevant and critical to understand if you work in an area where your services are specialist in nature and your customer base is small anyway. The loss of one customer when you have thousands is minimal, but if you can only cope with a few customers at a time, then losing one or more customers, without replenishing your customer stock, can have a dramatic effect.

In some businesses, moving from unqualified prospects (A) to buying customers (C) can take a long time. In some businesses, it can take up to 12 months to negotiate a buying contract. During that time, it would be extremely dangerous to stop prospecting activity (A), since it would have a knock-on effect eventually. Reducing the amount of prospecting activity in section 'A' in the short term would probably have little or no effect, other than slowly to reduce the number of qualified prospects (**Figure 12**).

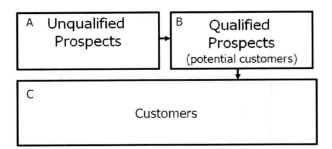

Figure 12: Prospects and Customers II: How Reducing Prospecting Affects the Number of Qualified Prospects

However, if you continued to reduce the amount of effort you put into finding new prospects and qualifying them into potential customers, the knock-on effect would be to reduce your buying customers (**Figure 13**).

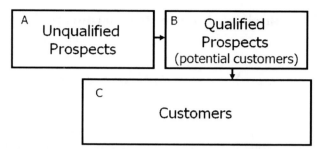

Figure 13: Prospects and Customers III: How Reducing Prospecting Eventually Affects the Number of Customers

The loss of a customer would have disastrous effects if the process of getting prospects from A to C took any considerable length of time. What normally happens is that a significant amount of effort then is placed into prospecting but, by this time, the customer base may have shrunk to the extent that it can no longer support the costs of running the business (**Figure 14**).

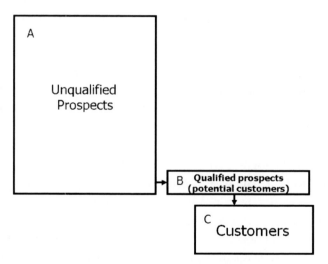

Figure 14: Prospects and Customers IV: Prospecting Activities Increased – But Too Late

The gap between prospecting and buying activity is crucial for any business or individual salesperson to understand. One the one hand, you can fool yourself into believing that you are very busy, but being busy does not pay the bills.

WHERE TO FIND PROSPECTS

Prospects are everywhere. It is possible to obtain or buy lists of prospects in your area. What you do with them is important, however. Suppose you obtain a list containing 100 names, postal and email addresses and telephone numbers of potential customers in your area, how would you go about contacting them in order to convert those names into possible sales leads? Does it matter how old the list is and whether any of your colleagues has already used it? Which is the most effective form of contact? What costs are involved in different methods of prospecting and is there any historical data available to help in constructing a cost-benefit analysis?

Then there is the time and cost involved in the process of preparing for and executing your prospecting plans. Spending an excessive amount of time in gathering information about prospects is pointless unless an approach is made. Salespeople who are not confident, however, tend to absorb themselves in administrative tasks to the exclusion of prospect contact. Eric Berne[30] said that this is known in transactional analysis terms as 'withdrawal', meaning that people whose natural tendency is to avoid people contact will seek occupations and tasks that require little human contact but large amounts of solitude. You may say that these people do not exist in sales roles, but my research shows that they are alive and well. A salesperson who is having a difficult time will use any method possible for showing that they are busy, whilst not actually selling face-to-face. The easiest activity for achieving this is prospecting, or at least the effort required in collecting possible prospect data. They learn this process on training courses where too much emphasis is placed on how to collect information, and not enough on how easy it is (and how dangerous it can be) to spend too much time on the process.

---

[30]   Berne, E. (1967). *Games People Play*, Harmondsworth: Penguin.

CONTACTING THE PROSPECT

Whatever amount of time you eventually dedicate to the gathering and collation of information, at some stage you will need to establish contact, but before you do that, there may be some issues you need to consider regarding communication.

Pre-Approach

If the point of making the first contact is to make an appointment, most salespeople pave the way by writing letters or sending emails to the prospect outlining their services, and saying that they will telephone for an appointment within the next few days. I used to do the same when I was less competent at using referred leads. If you are still cold-canvassing and using letters and emails as a way of your initial approach, the section on writing later will be of benefit to you. However, writing first is not always necessary. When you really analyse some of the costs, you can save yourself money by using the cheaper and far more effective option of asking for referrals. Some people, however, have a great deal of faith in pre-approach letters and emails.

I also have heard it suggested that one way to improve your chances of having the communication read is to have the chief executive, or another senior manager, sign the communication on your behalf. A format for this sort of approach might look like:

> Dear Mr. Brown,
>
> I would like to introduce you to a colleague of mine – (name). (Name) has been with my company for a number of years now, and I know that if you are able to spare him 15 minutes of your time, you will be as impressed with him as I am – etc, etc.

I think this is a terrific idea. Unfortunately, I have not heard of too many chief executives who have enough faith in their salespeople to do it. Your company might be different, and there is no harm in asking.

A less impressive suggestion once made to me was to send a communication that said that you would make a personal visit unless the customer telephones to cancel the appointment. Personally, I would not recommend this approach, but then it might work for you.

Whichever you choose, keep it brief and to the point. It could look like this:

Dear Mr Brown,

You have probably seen our promotional literature arrive on your desk from time to time. In most cases, I know from my other customers that it has to compete with thousands of other brochures and letters you probably receive. My belief is that the best way to make you fully aware of how my company can benefit you is to ask you for 15 minutes of your time. After which, if you have not heard anything new or interesting, I will leave. I will telephone you or your secretary within the next few days to arrange a suitably convenient appointment.

Make sure that when you write to someone saying that you will telephone, you do so within three or four days. Any longer, and the prospect either will have forgotten about you already or, if they were vaguely interested, will believe that you were not.

PERSONAL CALLING AND TELEPHONING

Personal calling

There always have been, and continue to be, salespeople who make personal calls on prospects, whether at their homes or businesses. Sometimes this works and sometimes it does not – it depends on the industry you are in. As a general rule of thumb, however, I recommend that you consider this option with great caution.

Whereas the strike rate for successful conversion from prospecting to a sale in direct marketing is on average 2%, strike rates for conversion from a prospect to a customer by knocking on the door is less than 0.1%. That means for every 1,000 doors you knock on, you might be lucky to convert only 1 person into a customer. In the meantime, you have probably suffered a considerable amount of indifference and possibly a significant amount of abuse.

Calling on a business without an appointment was a standard method of prospecting for a considerable time – certainly before widespread use of telecommunications. However, it is arguable whether the current habit of contact by email or telephone prior to a face-to-face encounter is more to do with salesperson reticence to possible rejection, buyer resistance to unannounced visits, or a combination of both. Calling without an appointment is certainly a very quick way to get feedback – though not all of it may be good.

I know of a number of salespeople, however, who use cold-calling as a very effective way of prospecting and qualifying, especially when the salesperson is new to a defined area. Visiting business premises tells you a lot more about the prospect than a telephone call, and certainly more than a business directory. I like the practice of some salespeople who use personal calling simply as a mechanism for finding out more information about a prospect, determining how best to get an appointment, and sometimes even gaining access. For example, you could call into a business, announce yourself, and simply state: "I was passing the door, and having noticed that 'company name' was based here, felt it would be a good idea to fix up a formal business appointment". Depending on who you speak to, you either get into describing what it is you do, and who you represent, manage to arrange an appointment, get a sale, or get thrown out! Either way, what is there to lose?

The trick with receptionists, secretaries, or any member of staff is to understand that they can be very helpful and are often treated disrespectfully by people who do not understand this. Simply ask: "Do you mind if I ask you for some help?" They will either say "Yes" or "It depends" – it is unlikely they will be rude enough on a first encounter to say "No" without hearing more. You then say, "I believe that my company/service will benefit your company, but what I need is a few minutes' time of the person responsible for making buying decisions. Tell me ...". And off you go.

Telephoning for an appointment

You could telephone to make an appointment, but what about the cost of telephone calls?[31] You might not get through first time, so do you write

---

[31] One way for this not to make a difference is to have a telephone contract that includes free calls as part of the package.

the prospect off or telephone back, thus increasing the cost? Your contact list might be out-of-date, which could mean that some of the names are no longer at the address/number given, or in the market for your product.

The telephone is extremely useful for making appointments to see customers. The secret of success however is 'ring up, fix up, shut up'. It is easy to get sidetracked, and be drawn into selling your product or service on the telephone. If you know that you are more successful when seeing people face-to-face, then you need to stick to a clear purpose which should be making the appointment. During the first few seconds of a call, you need to persuade your prospect that an appointment with you will be time well spent.

Having a script

Success using the telephone, more than any other form of selling, depends on good preparation, and the best way to prepare is to have a script. You need to know exactly what you want to say, how you want to say it, and how to respond when the customer says "No". If your story is good enough, most people will see you. However, you need to understand that saying "No" is a natural response.

A good standard opening script that I have used very successfully in the past was:

Mr/Mrs (name), good morning. This is (name) of (company). We recently launched a new service/product that I know someone like you would be interested in. I'd like the opportunity to discuss this personally with you in more detail. That's why I'm calling. I'll be in your area next week. Which is better for you Mr/Mrs (name), mornings or afternoons?

Customers sometimes come up with reasons, some very valid, for not agreeing to an appointment first time. However, you need to establish whether it is a valid 'show-stopping' reason, or perhaps just a conditioned response to all salespeople. Here are some common reasons given for not giving appointments, and how you might respond.

- **The customer says, "I'm not interested":** You say "I understand how you feel, Mr/Mrs (name). Most of my present customers initially said the same, and I certainly wouldn't expect you to be interested in something you haven't had the opportunity to see. But, after investing only 15 minutes, most felt it was a useful meeting. After that, it's up you whether you want to continue".

- **The customer says, "I haven't got any money":** You say, "I understand how you feel, Mr/Mrs (name). Most of my present customers initially said the same. However, as there is no commitment for you to buy anything, most felt it was a useful meeting. After that, it's up you whether you want to continue or not".

- **The customer says, "Send me a brochure":** You say, "Mr/Mrs (name), most of my present customers initially said the same. However, having now met with me, they understand that it was better to listen what I had to say face-to-face rather than reading brochures.

- **The customer says, "You are wasting your time":** You say, "Mr/Mrs (name), most of my present customers initially said the same. As the initial discussion would only take 15 minutes, however, most of them think now that it was time well spent".

- **The customer says, "Tell me about it now":** You say, "Mr/Mrs (name), most of my present customers initially said the same. They now feel it was better to have met face-to-face and as the initial discussion would only take 15 minutes to explain, most of them think now that it was time well spent".

- **The customer says, "I'm too busy":** You say, "Mr/Mrs (name), that's the reason I'm telephoning first rather than calling to see you without an appointment".

Alternatively, you could use this standard response, which I have found works on nearly all occasions: "Mr/Mrs (name), I can appreciate what you're saying. Many of my current customers gave a similar response when I first telephoned them. However, most of them are now pleased that they gave me 15 minutes of their time, and felt that the time was well spent".

Whichever response you choose, you should always end with: "Which is better for you Mr/Mrs (name), mornings or afternoons?"

If you sound confident, you will get an appointment. DO NOT, however, give the impression that you can see them anytime. Even if your diary is empty, you should give the customer the impression that you are busy, and you will try to fit them into your busy schedule. Nobody wants to see a salesperson with no other customers to see.

BUYING SIGNALS

Although I recommend using a script, the problem is that many salespeople become so intent on delivering each part of their prepared statement that they miss buying signals from the customer. There are times when this failure to recognise when the customer might want to buy or has already accepted your ideas actually can talk the customer into rejecting your product or service when previously they were reasonably interested in buying or at least to listening to more:

Salesperson: "Hello, Mr Smith, my name is Colin Jackson from Dixit".

Customer: "Ah, yes, I'm glad you phoned".

Salesperson: "Good. The reason for my call is to ask for a few minutes of your time".

Customer: "We've been thinking about changing our photo-copier equipment".

Salesperson: "Good. At Dixit, we have been developing a new approach to the marketing of our copiers, and there are a number of questions I would like to ask you. Do you currently have your own photo-copier?"

Customer: "I just said we have, but we are thinking of changing it".

Salesperson: "Good. Could you tell me, how long is there left on your contract?"

Customer: "I don't think that that's relevant. We want to change it".

Salesperson: "I can appreciate what you are saying. However, if we were able to show that by changing your copier now,

	we could save you a substantial amount on your copying costs, that would be of benefit, wouldn't it?"
Customer:	"Hello, hello, is this an answering machine I am speaking to?"

Exaggerated? Perhaps, and yet perhaps not. Sometimes in the pressure of making a call, obvious buying signals can be missed.

So what is a buying signal? A buying signal is something the prospect or customer says which indicates that they have a possible interest in or a desire to buy your product or service. Often, when a prospective customer is interested, they make a positive statement about your call, or ask you a positive question. In many cases, people do not come right out and say "Can I have it?" What they do is indicate their interest which, if handled properly, can and often does result in a sale.

Examples of verbal buying signals include:

- "Well, that could be of interest".
- "So how would that work?"
- "What sort of price would that be?"
- "Do you have that in another size?"
- "That sounds reasonable".
- "We have had problems with our current suppliers".
- "What's the delivery time on that?"

These are only a few examples and you can probably think about many more. Whether these signals turn into a sale lies in your ability to build upon one positive comment (and remember a question is a positive comment) by asking another question yourself aimed at either receiving an order or further agreement that your product matches the customer's requirements.

Suggested responses to some buying signals

- **"Well, that could be of interest"**: "In what way do you think that would help you?" or "What would make you decide to give us the opportunity of supplying you?"

- **"So how would that work?':** "How would you like it to work for you?" or "What in particular are you looking for?"
- **"What sort of price would that be?":** "Obviously, it depends on quantity/quality/delivery – what are you currently used to? And what's your main priority, price or quality/delivery/etc" (whatever your major selling point or unique selling point is).
- **"Do you have that in another size?":** "Which particular size are you interested in?"
- **"That sounds reasonable":** "What would make you buy it/change your current supplier?" or "What in particular do you like the sound of?"
- **"We have had problems with our current suppliers":** "So what would make you give someone like us an opportunity?"
- **"What's the delivery time on that?":** "What are you looking for?" or "If we can match that, would you like to proceed?"

If you are able to deliver at any time, it can be better to say, "Fortunately, because we are taking new deliveries every day, I can most probably supply that to meet your needs. When would you like it?"

SECRETARIES ARE NOT BARRIERS

Many salespeople assume that the main barrier to getting to see a decision-maker is the receptionist/secretary. It is further assumed that part of the secretary's remit is to keep people like you away from the boss. The reality is that it depends on who you are. If you are an annoying individual with nothing to say, then you could be right. When I was a buyer, there were certain people I did not want to speak to. Sometimes, it depended on whether I had any available budget or even the mood I was in. In either case, if you are in the business of building sales relationships, and you feel that you have something that genuinely will benefit the prospect, then you should not give up; find out when the best time would be to make your proposal.

Having said that, you need to work out what your best proposal would be, depending on what realistically you could achieve. For example, if you established that someone did not currently have a budget for your product, what is the point of selling it to him or her? What you could do is focus on your own personal strengths, and sell the next appointment. It is a curious thing but buyers rarely make what we would call 'rational decisions' about buying. They quickly forget the person who walked into their office two weeks ago with the ideal solution, but are more likely to buy something from the person who walks into their office next. That means you have to keep calling.

The person to help you do this is the receptionist/secretary. They are a great source of information and, contrary to popular belief, can help you to see the boss. I know a salesman who would deliver his presentation to the secretary prior to seeing the boss so that he got some useful feedback. You either can call in to see them face-to-face, or telephone them. I personally favour speaking to people face-to-face. The first thing you need to know is the buyer's name, and then the buyer's secretary's name. Quite often, the company's receptionist is willing to help you with this – for example, "I wonder if you could help me, please? I'm looking for some information so that I can write to the correct person in your company". Then ask for the name of the person responsible for buying your product, their job title, and the name and job title of their secretary. Make absolutely sure that you also ask how to spell their names. When you are ready, you can call again, and perhaps you could try the following approach:

Hello. Can you put me through to Linda Smith, please? I believe that she is Peter Brown's secretary. Is that right?'

Hello, is that Linda Smith? Linda, my name is (name) and I work for (company). Linda, I wonder if you could help me, please?

Tell me, are you Peter Brown's secretary?

Linda, I'm putting together a letter to Peter about my company. I just wanted to make absolutely sure that I have his job title correct, as well as spelling his name properly.

My company provides training and consultancy services to organisations such as yours. Am I right in thinking that Peter is the person responsible for buying these sorts of services?

Linda, I know how busy Peter must be, and he probably only scans most of the mail that arrives on your desk on inbox, let alone take time to see the people who want to make appointments with him. My problem is that I know I can help your company to improve its profits. However, the only way I can effectively explain how is to take 15 to 20 minutes of Peter's time. That's why I wanted to write to him first. In your experience, what would I have to say in my letter/email that would convince him that I am worth seeing when I ring up a few days later to make an appointment?'

Take it slowly. Look and sound sincere (that is why it is better to do this face-to-face). It is important that you practice this approach until you are word perfect.

If the prospect is not in, and the secretary suggests that you leave your number, and he or she will call you back, say, "When would be the best time to speak to (name)?" You need to establish when next to call, and when the chances are favourable for getting through to the decision-maker. Relying on the customer to ring you back rarely works unless they know you personally.

When you have established a good time to call, say, "Would you put my name in (name's) diary and say that I will telephone at that time?"

Alternatively, ask to be put through to the customer's voice mail, and leave a message yourself saying when you will call back.

A good idea also might be to send a brief email saying that you have called, and when you will telephone back. It is also worth mentioning that you will only need three minutes of their time, after which it is up to them if they want to continue or not. Everyone can spare three minutes, but if you say 'a few minutes', then they also assume it will take ages.

NEXT ...

- Conduct a workload analysis for yourself. What are your conclusions?

- What sources could you use to identify prospects for your product/service?

- How long would it take for a lack of prospecting to affect your income?

CHAPTER 6

BASIC COMMUNICATION IN SELLING

SUMMARY

- A simple communication model focuses on an analysis of stimulus and response elements.
- Open and closed questions, whilst easy to define, are less workable in reality.
- Often, it is not what you say that counts, but how you say it.
- A study of body language is must for all sales professionals.

Ask most people what the most important thing in selling is, and they probably will say determination, perseverance, commitment, or the like. Whilst it may be true, being in possession of all of these traits, without having the basic skill of communication, counts for nothing. It is the ability to communicate effectively that makes some people able to sell more than others. Those who are successful communicate their ideas better than those who are unsuccessful. One sales message, transmitted by two different people, can have two different outcomes.

WHAT IS COMMUNICATION?

First, it is a two-way process. Communication cannot have been said to have taken place until a message has been sent and received. Messages can be received but, if they are either misunderstood or not understood at all, they can be worthless. Second, the message has to be understood. Without understanding, there is confusion and, potentially, mistrust.

Communication in selling can be defined as:

The sharing of information/ideas/or attitudes between a customer and a salesperson by words, tone or behaviour, which leads to a greater understanding of the needs of both, and which enhances the buyer/seller relationship.

STIMULUS AND RESPONSE

In successful selling, the main component is good communication. In simple terms, there are two basic elements to communication (**Figure 15**):

- **Stimulus:** The information which is sent, and which therefore begins the communication event.

- **Response:** The way in which the information is received, which produces the reply.

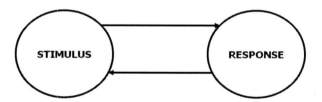

Figure 15: Communication I: Stimulus + Response

On the surface, this appears straightforward. Practitioners of Neuro Linguistic Programming (NLP) believe that a potential barrier to effective communication is that you might not be offering the customer the information in their preferred format (**Figure 16**), the options for which are:

- **Audio:** A preference for hearing information.
- **Visual:** A preference for seeing information.
- **Kinaesthetic:** A preference for feeling information.

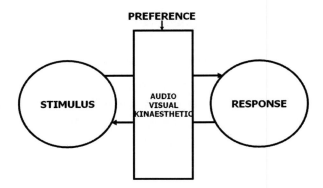

Figure 16: Communication II: The NLP Approach

In addition, NLP practitioners argue that you should take time to test which format the customer prefers to receive information by providing it in all three formats. Then through observation, listening to responses (**Figure 17**), and through general analysis, you arrive at the ideal format.

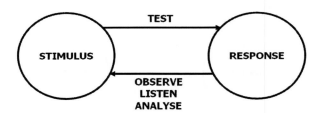

Figure 17: Communication III: Testing for the Ideal NLP Format

Again, NLP practitioners believe that you can tell from a person's eye movements which is their preferred communication channel: auditory, visual or kinaesthetic (**Figure 18**).

When people look upward, they are seeing a picture in their mind's eye. Looking up to the right or left means that they are looking for visual images. Looking to the left or right means that they are attempting to recall something they heard. Looking down to the right means that they are trying to recall a particular feeling. The theory is that you then copy their eye movements and 'hey presto', the sale is won.

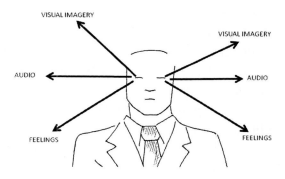

Figure 18: Communication IV: Eye Movements Identify a Preference for Communication Channel

This might work if you have a lot of time, or a degree in psychology. A simpler way is to accept that, from time to time, there can be barriers between what you want to say, and what is received. You may think your message has been conveyed accurately, but because of differing perceptions, the emotional state of the receiver, or their past experiences (**Figure 19**), the understanding your customer might have could be totally different from the one you intended, and therefore they respond unexpectedly.

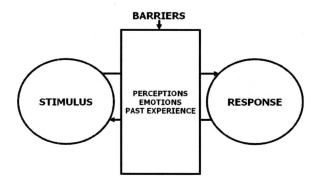

Figure 19: Communication V: Barriers

For example, you might say that your product is cheap, meaning it to be good value for money, whereas the customer might equate 'cheap' with poor quality. Words can mean different things to different people. Your customer might have recently experienced an emotional upset and, if they have something else on their mind whilst you are trying to sell to them, you could have the greatest product in the world, but you might not be getting an effective hearing.

This is why you need to be able to concentrate on the customer whilst delivering your opening statements. By observing their response, you will know whether they are with you or not. You cannot hope ever to psychoanalyse them, or to prepare 1,001 different ways of delivering your message based on whether they fit into one particular mindset or another. All you can hope for is to make the best presentation you can, based upon what I know works for most people:

- Story-telling.

- Involvement through questioning (but not interrogation).

STORY-TELLING

One of the most effective ways to get and hold anyone's attention is to communicate by story-telling. We all love to hear stories and, when they contain details about other people, especially those we have heard of or know personally, they can make a tremendous impact. In many older civilisations, the storyteller in the community was held in very high esteem, especially in those communities where the written word was not used. Even in civilisations where history was recorded in some written form, the storyteller played an important role in bringing history to life. Although it might not appear evident in a world where computer games, videos, and television seems to play such an important part in children's lives, story-telling still remains a captivating activity. Even the most popular computer games are based on story-telling, otherwise they would be a relatively pointless activity.

Most children, if caught young enough, prefer hearing and experiencing a live story rather than the less interactive process of watching television. It remains a fact that our imaginations are far more inventive than virtual reality. Stories help us to retain information and, if you are in competition with other salespeople selling similar products to yours, then in most cases the customer will tend to be influenced by who impressed them most.

Whenever I am training salespeople, I make them deliver a number of presentations on many different subjects. I guarantee that the only presentations that are both memorable and enjoyable are those which contain personal stories.

Your opening story should not be longer than three to four minutes. Any longer, and it can become boring. All of us like listening to stories, but we also like to be involved in conversation. Therefore, immediately following your brief story, you need to begin the process of involving your customer. Many salespeople I have met have the idea that the only way to sell is to ask lots of questions, and whilst I do not disagree with the need to ask questions, I am less convinced that opening sales conversations with questions helps. In many instances where I have observed a salesperson begin a sales interview with a question, I have seen the customer almost take a step backwards. At the very least, they feel under pressure.

Telling a story at the beginning of a sales presentation puts the customer at ease, and helps them to decide whether you sound interesting enough to listen to the sales proposal, which brings me to the next point. Some people have said that they do not see the point of story-telling, the assumption being that you become jaded telling the same old story, and eventually become and sound boring. They miss the point. First, the customer has never heard your story before – if they have, then tell another one. Second, professional actors tell the same old story every night on the stage. They do not become boring because what they try and do is to perform it better every time. The problem with making up and telling a different story every time is that you will always sound like an amateur. The difference between salespeople who achieve regular success, and those who do not, usually can be found in the differences that are evident in their story-telling ability. Top salespeople have a way of expressing what they do for a living that sounds interesting.

Most important, however, is when you develop your opening story, make certain it is relevant to the business you are in and the reason for you being there.

ASKING QUESTIONS

I keep six honest serving-men
(They taught me all I knew);
Their names are What and Why and When
And How and Where and Who.
The Elephant's Friend, Rudyard Kipling

Open and closed questions
In most sales books and on nearly all sales training events, the subject of questioning technique inevitably comes up. Asking questions is certainly a vital ingredient of any sales process. There is, however, a naïve assumption that there are two main categories of questions which, when used, will determine either success or failure in the sale. Those from the Rudyard Kipling quotation above are supposed to be open questions.

Using the words What, Where, When, Who, How, and Why as a prefix to a sentence indeed might elicit a response, and on occasions, encourage the customer to speak readily. They may be useful in general conversation. Yet it is also possible to use these prefixes and receive very short answers, which is what closed questions are supposed to stimulate – for example:

- Q: "What are you looking for?"

  A: "Nothing".

- Q: "When did you want it delivered?"

  A: "I don't".

- Q: "Where to?"

  A: "Here".

- Q: "Who will collect them?"

  A: "Me".

- Q: "How do you want them packaged?"

A: "Gift-wrapped".

- Q: "Why would that be a problem?"

  A: "It just is".

Closed questions, on the other hand, are those that are answered with a "No" or a "Yes". But again, this may not be the case always – for example:

- Q: "Would you like some?"

  A: "What if I wanted a different colour?"

- Q: "Can I take that order now, please?"

  A: "Do you mind if I ring my partner up and check something out first?"

- Q: "Is there anything wrong?"

  A: "What do you mean?"

The problem is that customers do not go to the same training courses as salespeople do, and very often they will answer "Yes" or "No" to an open question, or drone on endlessly in response to a closed question. Have you ever been on an aeroplane or a train, and without asking the person next to you a question, they begin a one-sided conversation? Alternatively, you must have encountered a number of individuals who, even if you pleaded with them, would not respond to Kipling's serving-men. The best of salespeople I know could not tell you the difference between an open question and a closed question – but it is not what they say that matters, it is how they say it.

You can go home, and in passing say, "Had a busy day?" Depending on how you say it, and how your wife/husband/partner hears it, this simple comment can have a multitude of outcomes. Even if you say it in the nicest way possible, it is not guaranteed to bring the expected response. When someone has said to you at work "This is no criticism of you personally", did you believe them? And what then happened? They probably started to criticise you.

Words alone mean very little. That is part of the problem with the assumption that a question is open or closed, simply by the way in which it is constructed. It is not the type of question that matters, but the way in which the question is asked. All successful salespeople are good at asking questions. It comes naturally to them, or so it would seem, and yet the only way to learn the skill is to practise it constantly.

Types of questions

Table 1 shows a range of question types collated by Lancaster and Jobber,[32] together with a brief explanation of the objective of asking the question, and an example:

Question Type	Objective	Example
Tie down	Used for confirmation or to commit a prospect to a position.	You want the program to work don't you?
Leading	Direct or guide a prospect's thinking.	How does that coat feel on you?
Alternative	Used to elicit an answer by forcing selection from two or more alternatives.	Would you prefer the red or the blue model?
Statement/Question	A statement is followed by a question that forces the prospect to reflect upon the statement.	This machine can spin at 500 rpm and process three units per minute. What do you think of that productivity?
Sharp angle	Used to commit a prospect to a position.	If we can get it in blue, is that the way you would want it?
Information-gathering	Used to gather facts.	How many people do you currently employ?
Confirmation	Used to elicit either agreement or disagreement about a particular topic.	Do my recommendations make sense?
Clarification	Reduce ambiguities, generalities and non-committal words to specifics.	When you say ... exactly what do you mean?
Inclusion	Present an issue for the prospect's consideration in a low-risk way.	I don't suppose you'd be interested in a convertible hardtop, would you?
Counter-biasing	To attain sensitive information by making potentially embarrassing situations appear acceptable.	Research shows that most drivers exceed the speed limit. Do you ever do so?

---

[32] Lancaster, G. and Jobber, D. (1990). *Sales: Technique & Management*, Philadelphia, PA: Pitman.

Question Type	Objective	Example
Transitioning	Used to link the end of one phase to the next phase of the sales process.	In addition to that, is there anything else that you want to know? (No) What I'd like to do now is talk about ...
Reversing	Used to pass the responsibility of continuing the conversation back to the prospect by answering a question with a question.	(When can I expect delivery?) When do you want delivery?

Table 1: Question Types, Objectives and Examples

Rhetorical questions

Perhaps you should not leave the answer you want to chance. You could use rhetorical questions, which are the sort where you give the answer yourself. In some textbooks, it is said that rhetorical questions have no need for an answer, and that no response from the customer means "Yes". Without stating the obvious, the sort of rhetorical questions you could use are: "In my experience, Mr Doyle, most people are looking for something that's reliable, and that's probably the same for you?"

Notice the question mark at the end of the sentence, which means you should raise your voice at the end to suggest a question. You can ask a question simply by the sound of your voice, not just by constructing a grammatically correct question.

Tom Hopkins[33] suggests we should use tie-downs, which to all intents and purposes are open questions, but better, in that they invite people to respond. Examples of tie-downs are:

- "Isn't it?"
- "Don't you?"
- "Haven't you?"
- "Can't we?"
- "Isn't that right?"
- "Don't you agree?"

---

[33] Hopkins, T (1983). *How To Master the Art of Selling*, London: Grafton Books.

There are hundreds of these, and you can have great fun role-playing with your colleagues a game which involves everyone talking to each other but with the strict rule that you must end each sentence with a tie-down. In this way, the conversation can go on endlessly until someone either gives up or tires. It is a bit like the Yes/No interlude on the 1960s game show, *Take Your Pick*,[34] where contestants had to last a minute without saying "Yes" or "No" whilst Michael Miles asked them endless questions, some open, some closed.

If you use tie-downs, be careful about over-use. As you will find out from the role-play game, it can be infuriating to be faced always with another question after you have answered one or even asked one yourself. Customers could become very irritated.

Hopkins also recommends sometimes swapping the tie-down to the front of sentence. Examples of both types follow:

- "Mr Doyle, if I could show you how to save money you'd be interested wouldn't you?"
- "Mr Doyle, you'd be interested, wouldn't you, if I could show you a way to save money?"

WRITING TO CUSTOMERS

Producing good sales letters and emails is an industry in itself, and best left to professional writers. At the same time, I know that most companies have standard letters and emails that salespeople can use. I also know that most salespeople insist on composing their own. Not only does it waste valuable selling time, but also it is a completely pointless exercise. What do you think customers do with letters and emails? As soon as they know it is a sales letter or email, they stop paying attention to it, and bin it or delete it. It may not be scientific but I have noticed over the years that the salespeople who looked the busiest were not necessarily the most successful. It strikes me that perhaps they thought they were busy because they were always working at something. The successful salespeople were nowhere to

---

[34] http://www.youtube.com/watch?v=irg29je8G8k,
      http://www.youtube.com/watch?v=irg29je8G8k

be seen. They were to be found in front of customers! Use the services of people within your company who are good at writing and save your time for selling to people face-to-face.

A sales letter is usually a precursor to the sender taking some action – for example, "I will telephone you in the next few days in order to make an appointment to meet up with you", or inviting the recipient to respond to an offer in the letter – for example, "If you would like to take advantage of this offer please call me on 03457 100100".

Both types are dependent upon whether the customer perceives the service or product offered as matching their needs at that particular time, or even whether the customer bothers to read the letter at all. Most people, inundated with advertising from every conceivable source, are able to spot direct marketing letters and emails either before they are opened, or as soon as they open them, and they discard them without a further glance. So what you have to consider when deciding to write to an existing customer or a prospective customer is what will make this person take any notice of the content of this communication? The objective is to grab the customer's attention.

What makes written communication worth reading?
The first thing we normally consider when a letter or email arrives is "Is this for me?" We tend to respond better to communication when it contains our first names. Whatever way you begin, your aim should be to establish common ground between you and the customer. In the way that in face-to-face communication each party looks for common ground before deciding that effective communication is happening, the same happens in written communication. The purpose presumably is to get the prospect or customer to do something that they are currently not doing – which may be to buy something from you that they are not buying, or to meet with you, when they have not instigated the meeting. That is to say, you want them to change their behaviour, or to increase their buying behaviour, which is the same thing. The question they will be asking themselves is "Why bother?"

You need to be able to put yourself in the customer's place, and think about how they might respond to a letter, before you start writing letters to customers. You have to see the thing from their point of view, not yours. On one level, people could argue that you start off from differing perspectives: you want to sell; they do not want to buy. However, this may not be true. They might want to buy something but do not know where from, or perhaps they are concerned about value for money. You might be selling just what they want at a price they believe is reasonable, and therefore satisfying your own needs, whilst at the same time, satisfying theirs.

Sell the sizzle not the sausage!
Hidden in everything you want to sell is the sizzle – the reason why someone would want to listen to your sales story, or want to buy your product. This is never more true than when writing to a prospect or a customer. You have very little space or time to sell them the idea that it is worth their while continuing to read the rest of the communication.

Facts not opinions
Unless you really know for certain that you are on the same wavelength as your customer, begin with facts, not opinions – for example, "55% of people in this country will retire at aged 65 reliant upon state handouts", rather than "We think it's important to think about investing for your retirement". Then back it up with a reference – the more independent the better. This means that, if you believe that your product is better that anything else out there, find some research to back it up. When you are testing a new product line with a small number of customers, make sure that part of the deal of any reduced introductory offer is that customers will provide you with a testimonial that you will be allowed to use in a promotional letter.

How does it apply to the prospect?
The next stage is to have the prospect consider whether a) the facts are pertinent to themselves, and b) whether you might be the person to satisfy a need that up until now they did not know they had – for example, "If this is the same for you, then you might consider doing something about it". The prospect also will be expecting you to be

selling them something, therefore it is important for you to show some objectivity by briefly presenting other possibilities – for example, "You may be expecting to supplement your shortfall in retirement income by continuing to work or perhaps you have an expectation of an inheritance". And then leave your own proposal as possibly the more favoured option, again backed up by research from other people – for example, "However, what our other customers like you have said is that they would prefer to be in control of their own lives".

Promotional offers

In order to stimulate initial activity, you might consider making a promotional offer. You need to consider, however, whether a promotional offer of a discount or a free gift could detract from the value of your service or product. If you are selling at a premium to a small market, will the effect of discounting affect future price potential, or even upset existing buyers who have bought at a higher price?

Research has shown[35] that up to 60% of the population in the UK had taken part in some form of promotional activity in any given month – whether by entering a competition, sending in for a free gift, or using money-off coupons. The success of this type of activity increases dramatically when combined with television advertising. Yet, you do not need to go to the expense of television advertising to benefit from its effect. If your product or service is similar to something being advertised on the television, you might be able to 'piggy-back' – for example, "You might have seen some television advertising recently talking about the damage that hard water can do to your plumbing system. We have just launched a new product ...".

FEATURES, BENEFITS, AND LEFT-BRAIN ACTIVITY

It is said that customers are not interested in what products and services *are*, only in what they *do*. If you are selling tangible products

---

[35]   Harris International Marketing (1986). *Marketing Weekly*.

such as a car, stereo equipment, or stationery, then you certainly can say that customers really only are interested in what your product or services will do for them. Do people buy drills or the holes they make?

On that basis, it should be relatively easy to look at a product feature and convert it into a customer benefit:

- "This car has a 2-litre engine. What that means for you is that driving is smoother, and you can overtake safely".

- "This stereo has a 50-watt output. In other words, you don't have to turn the volume up to get a really good quality sound".

- "This new computer has a super fast chip, and what this means for you is that you can process your work in half the time it takes you to do it now".

- "The price of the new chocolate bar has been increased but so has the size, and the benefit to you will be increased turnover".

Take a piece of paper and draw a line down the middle, dividing it into two. On the left-hand side write down a feature, and then on the right-hand side, ask the question, "What does this do for the customer?"

Applying straightforward features and benefits principles when selling intangibles, however, such as consultancy or insurance is more complicated. Begin by adopting the principle just discussed:

- "This policy includes a waiver of premium, which means that if you fall ill and cannot pay, then the insurance company will not cancel the policy".

- "You will get a refund if anything goes wrong; in other words, you will still be able to enjoy that holiday of a lifetime".

By changing features to benefits, you are attempting to appeal to the area of the brain that deals with emotion (**Figure 20**). In general terms, we tend to make emotional rather than logical buying decisions. We use logic to reinforce our buying decisions, but we buy things because we like them. If this were not the case, 95% of the economy would be non-existent and the only trade would be in food, animal skins, water carriers, and matches! In other words, we use the right side of the brain to make such decisions and the left side to justify them.

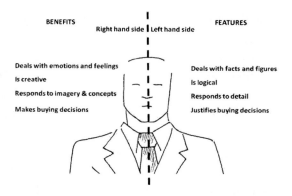

Figure 20: Benefits and Features Appeal to Different Parts of the Brain

Converting features to benefits, especially for intangibles, is more complicated than some make it out to be. Let us examine an example from the insurance industry. I have found that there are enormous lessons to be learned from the selling of these complicated intangibles that are pertinent to everyone in sales.

Surveys have shown that the overwhelming majority of the general public has a total non-understanding of insurance and pensions. When it comes to specific products such as unit trusts and investment trusts, consumer understanding is even less. Recently when 2,000 people were asked whether they understood the difference between a unit trust and an investment trust, 70% said they did not know, 15% said they did, and a further 15% didn't understand the question!

In another piece of research, a major financial institution surveyed 1,000 of their borrowers, who were asked whether they understood what type of mortgage they had: 80% replied that they had a repayment mortgage – in fact, 70% had an endowment mortgage. Of those that understood that they had an endowment mortgage, 65% believed the endowment policy was a product of the lender – this particular financial institution sold products of a third party introducer. People had no idea what they were being sold, and this was in relation to the biggest debt of their lives! Whose fault was it? It could be an all too common problem of communication. There are many industries that appear to have their own language.

Learning and sales training in many industries is concerned with the acquisition of product knowledge and, given the first opportunity, salespeople up and down the country share that knowledge with anyone unfortunate enough to be trapped into listening to them. The customer nods, and mumbles, and says "Oh yes" and "Aha", so that on the outside everything seems normal.

People are not interested in the product itself but in what the product does, whether it is a tangible product like a car, or an intangible product such as insurance. Even luxury items that people buy, which seem to have no use, are bought for reasons of status. Nobody buys designer label goods because they really believe they are worth the extra, do they?

So how does this affect your sales proposal? In simple terms, a feature is something that means something to you – but means absolutely nothing to the customer. Your problem is that internally, in the company, all you are taught and talk about is features. A benefit is said to be what a particular product feature does for a customer. However, I must caution you at this stage: carrying out this exercise will only highlight your perception of a customer benefit and not what the customer thinks, and the two could be worlds apart.

Think about a product such as term assurance. A feature of term assurance is that it is for a fixed term. A benefit for the customer is that they can have cover for a specific period of need. But so what? You need to take this to the next stage by detailing how you would describe this to a customer. You might be right about the benefit, but unless you can get the customer to understand and to personally identify with the benefit, it will be as interesting as the feature was. It is very easy to describe a feature; with training, it is relatively easy to describe a benefit. But if you simply leave the description of your product or service as what it does, then customers rightfully do not have a clue what it is you are talking about.

Also, many people are too embarrassed to ask the salesperson what they mean, or to say that they do not understand. Even when the salesperson says, "Do you understand?", customers always say "Yes". We are all conditioned to say "Yes" when we are asked "Do you understand?" When you were at school, and the teacher asked "Do you understand?", what did you say? I am sure that you said "Yes" – and why? Because you did not want to appear stupid, or get into trouble for not understanding. We are taught quite early on that having learning difficulties is not normal. So just because customers nod their heads and appear to understand what you are saying, it is no guarantee that they do.

So where does this leave you? You need to find another way either of checking understanding or of establishing that the customer has not understood. It is usually better to take the blame first: "Mr Doyle, at this stage I usually find that in my enthusiasm for the product, I have a tendency to either confuse people or fail to check for understanding. So that I do not make that mistake again, can I just ask you – the benefit that I just mentioned about the pro-logical surround sound feature – is that of interest to you, or does it not mean a lot to you?" In this way, the customer is more likely to admit a lack of understanding, and it allows you to reassure them if they do by saying: "That's my fault, Mr Doyle. I just get carried away, and because I work with the product every day, I assume everyone else is as excited about it as I am".

After you have converted the product feature into a customer benefit, you need to find a way of describing it that paints a picture in the customer's mind. Inevitably, customers buy based on emotional triggers that are engaged through an image they see, hear or feel internally. We use emotion to buy, and logic to reinforce our buying decision.

So how can you best explain the benefit of having insurance cover for a specific period? It is advisable to use a simple phrase to help the customer understand an important point about your product or service. Some of the simple linking phrases you can use are:

- "What this means for you is ..."
- "In other words ..."

- "Putting it another way ..."
- "The benefit to you is ..."
- "What that means is ..."
- "The good thing about that is ..."
- "What people like about that is ..."

And so on.

Returning to the intangible term assurance: "What this product does is to give you security for a specific period. This means that you have peace of mind when you need it". This description is all right so far as it goes, and many of you probably have reached this stage during some sales training session or other. Many of you also know that when you come to use it in a real sales situation, it often does not work.

Let us look at that phrase again: "What this product does is to give you security for a specific period. This means that you have peace of mind when you need it". The problem is that the customer cannot see security, cannot see a specific period, and cannot see peace of mind. These are words, and people cannot recall words – only in songs, poems, or famous lines and quotes, such as from films. If you sing your presentation, the outcome may be different, but it is about the only way that you will get people to remember the words.

Consider the key points of that phrase again: 'security', 'specific period', 'peace of mind'. What do you see when you think of security? A wall, a fence, security lights, a bodyguard? The idea of security could be synonymous with putting a fence around yourself. Picture it in your mind and then describe it. What colour is it? What material? How big? Perhaps a better way to describe these benefits would be, "I look on this sort of policy as a big wooden fence, built to protect your family against the elements. As it is temporary, we have decided not to make it a brick wall, and in that way it is cheaper, but still effective, for the job you had in mind". Better?

COMMUNICATION PROBLEMS

Nearly all of the problems in the world are brought about through a lack of effective communication. How many times have you heard, "I speak but they just don't listen" or "I've written to them a number of times, but I have had no reply" or "It's obvious they don't want to communicate with me" or "If only someone asked me, I would tell them".

The biggest problem with communication is that we believe that it is an inherent skill, and therefore do it without thinking. This lulls us into thinking that we know how to communicate, and so we seldom take the opportunity to improve the way in which we do so. Communication is a skill, and as such has to be learned, and can be improved.

We speak the language we do because we have been taught it, both formally in classrooms, and informally at home and at work. Putting it all together is a learned, and learnable, skill. That is the easy part, but what about the down-side? You might be able to speak English, but does anybody understand the English you speak? Is your English clear? Does it matter?

In selling, if you are up against competition, if the conditions of the sale are equal, but the way in which you describe your product is confusing, and the way in which a competitor describes the same product is understandable, who will get the business?

To succeed at selling, you need to create a situation where the deck is stacked in your favour. It is difficult enough without giving the competition a head-start.

Sometimes, communication is made more difficult because of the following barriers:

- The way in which you articulate yourself.
- The speed with which you speak.
- Your body language, which could be misread.
- The customer does not listen to you.
- Your written communication can be misunderstood or lost.
- You might sound insincere.

- Your description of your product or service is ambiguous.
- The customer's description of their needs is ambiguous.
- You or the customer have something else on your mind at the time of the meeting.
- Either you or the customer are not motivated enough to communicate.
- You may dislike the customer, or they may dislike you.
- You might not be cut out to sell in the first place.

I am sure that you easily could come up with many more. But the key point is that you should not take communication for granted.

TRUST

If people do not trust you, they will not buy. Most long-term sales relationships are based upon trust. Customers trust salespeople they can communicate with. People buying your product rarely want to know how it works. When you go home and switch on the light, it does not bother you how it works. You pay the bill for the electricity with complete and utter faith and trust that others have got it right, and they are charging you for the correct amount. You do not question how the meter works or how the electricity works. When you last bought fuel for your car, did you test the fuel before you put it into the car? You are totally dependent on whatever the sign says is actually there, before you put it into your car. You never, ever question that you are getting what you pay for. Why? Because you have implicit trust in the people selling you the petrol. If people are not buying from you, then they probably do not trust you.

RAPPORT[36]

Perhaps it is a personal thing but I find the whole subject of rapport-building extremely annoying, and pointless. Talking to customers in the opening few minutes of your sales presentation about totally

---

[36] http://en.wikipedia.org/wiki/Rapport

unrelated topics insults the customer, and demeans what you do for a living. The customer is not stupid, and will recognise what you are doing. They rarely say, "Why on earth are you prattling on about the weather? Why have you come to see me?", but that is exactly what they think.

The concept of rapport-building is a common theme amongst salespeople and sales trainers. In many sales organisations, it usually expresses itself in the form of finding something interesting to talk about when first meeting a customer. Typically, this might mean making a mental note of the customer's premises or home, as you park your car. If it is the latter, then you are supposed to demonstrate that you are a keen gardener too. You could note the make and model of the car parked outside so that you can show that you also are a Mercedes/Vauxhall/Citroen/Skoda fan. If the worst comes to the worst, you can always talk about the pottery ducks flying up the mantelpiece in order to show that you too are a very sad person!

The rationale behind this process is that it is supposed to:

- Put the customer at ease.
- Show the customer that you have something in common with them.

Objective research done in this area[37] suggests that the primary hidden agenda of salespeople who habitually conduct rapport-building is to put themselves at ease, rather than the customer, and that the more time spent in small talk, the lower the customer's regard for the salesperson.

Successful sales people have neither the time, nor the need for such devices. True rapport building consists of presenting yourself and the services you offer in a professional, confident and competent manner. It is these behaviours that people buy, not your ability to talk meaningfully about ducks, daffodils or Land Rovers.

---

[37] Gellerman, S.W. (1990). 'The tests of a good salesperson', *Harvard Business Review*, May-June.

NEXT ...

- What can you do to improve your basic communication skills?
- How could you improve your ability to 'read' body language?
- Commit yourself to recording and listening to your voice at least once per month.

CHAPTER 7

USING THE TELEPHONE

SUMMARY

- You need to focus on how to replace the 'visual' medium of communication when using the telephone.
- Develop and use word pictures.
- Smile when you dial.
- The only way to know how you come across on the telephone is to record your voice.
- People do not turn you down, they turn your message down.
- If you are making appointments on the telephone – ring up, fix up, shut up.

Since the telephone was invented, it has become an essential method of communication between most people. That said, the advent of email, text messaging, and social networking gradually but inexorably has taken over as a primary means of communication amongst younger age groups. Yet even texting requires a telephone, albeit a mobile. The telephone remains a primary tool for salespeople. Either they take calls from customers or they use the telephone to contact people in order to sell to customers.

Communicating effectively by telephone involves the Three Ps:

- Positive Mental Attitude (PMA).
- Preparation.
- Physical practice.

POSITIVE MENTAL ATTITUDE

Positive mental attitude usually determines whether telephone calls have successful outcomes for salespeople. Whether making or receiving calls, without training, the sales success of the call relies on luck. With training, sales success rates can be improved greatly. The problem for most people is that they make assumptions about their ability to use the telephone, simply because it is such an everyday object. Think about how much training you may have had in its use. We often assume that we can use it without training simply because we can speak. We receive a few instructions about its operation, and because we can talk, find ourselves using the telephone very quickly, but rarely effectively, especially as salespeople. It is no different to driving a car. You see other people doing it, it looks relatively easy, and the explanation of pushing a couple of pedals and turning a wheel looks simple enough. Without instruction, however, we soon find ourselves in trouble driving a car. In a sales sense, the same thing happens. Sales can be lost, sometimes without even noticing, simply because we do not prepare enough, we do not practice enough, and that is all because we have the wrong attitude in the first place.

Everyone has bad days. We all get out of bed on the wrong side from time to time. It happens usually on those days when we have an important call to make or there is a major campaign starting and we have to be at our best. No matter how you may be feeling, it is important to recognise the fact that behaviour breeds behaviour. A person who makes it apparent that they are in a bad mood will inflict this mood on others and soon everyone can be in a bad mood. On the telephone, it is very difficult for you to hide how you are feeling. The golden rule, therefore, before starting to either make or receive calls is to get yourself in the right frame of mind. For some people that means listening to music, some people read something inspirational, others just take a few minutes out to relax and prepare themselves mentally. So far as the people at the other end of the telephone are concerned, they have their own problems, one of which might be you, so they are not interested in sharing your concerns.

When successful salespeople use the telephone, they adopt the following processes and mindset:

- They spend as much time prior to the call getting themselves prepared (physically and mentally), as they do on making calls.

- They always choose the right environment in which to make their calls.

- They use a script that they know works every time.

- If they are making appointments, they offer the prospect alternative appointment times – for example, morning or afternoon? Wednesday or Thursday?

- They practice.

- They believe that their potential customers will not have any objection to seeing them, once they explain the benefits of meeting.

- They believe that any refusal to grant an appointment is not aimed at them, but at the past inadequate performance of other poorly trained salespeople.

If you are telephoning people, you should understand that they want to answer the telephone in the expectation that the call is for them. It is a fact that no matter what we are doing, we will stop in order to answer the telephone. This means that a person's initial reaction to your call is positive. The only time this changes is if they hear something from you that changes their perception.

The flip side of positive expectations is the expectation you have of yourself, the call, and your performance. It is the fear of rejection that affects most salespeople's voices. Failure in telephone selling is in the mind. If you think that there is a chance of the customer saying "No", it will come across in your voice, and they *will* say "No".

PREPARATION

Creating the right environment for making telephone calls
There is a lot to be said for making calls in a quiet room with no distractions, and yet many telesales organisations find that making calls with your peers around you helps to sustain motivation and positive attitude. The trick is to find out what works best for you. Whatever the external surrounding, however, the most important

thing is to get the internal environment right, and the near external environment professionally organised.

Have everything to hand

Being well-organised is crucial in telephone selling. You need to have everything within easy reach. Make sure you have enough pens or pencils handy so that if one runs out you have a replacement. Do not rely on scraps of paper for messages. Use a standard system which may already be provided by the company or develop one of your own.

PRACTICE

Replacing the visual

We have five major senses: sight, sound, touch, smell and taste. Depending on the situation, we use all of these to a greater or lesser extent. When we use the telephone, we are deprived of nearly all of these sources, apart from sound. There is good news and bad news in that. The good news is that, if we take all five senses together and were to analyse which is most effective in communication terms, touch, taste, and smell score very low (**Figure 21**).

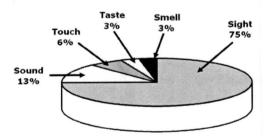

Figure 21: The Five Senses Used in Communication

The bad news is that sight scores a hefty 75%. If you consider that television and the internet represents for many people the main media for receiving information about what is happening in the world, then communication is all about visual reception. Like most people, you are able to gauge what is going on by what you see and less by what you hear. You have no doubt heard the phrase 'seeing is believing' and that is why most people tend to believe what they see on television and on the internet.

It is a well-known fact that face-to-face communication relies heavily on the three main channels of:

- Body language.
- Tone of voice.
- The words we use.

Unless you use something such as the video facility on Skype, or videoconferencing, then all that will be left to you when you use the telephone is the words that you use, and the tone of your voice. On the face of it, this represents less than 20% of effective communication channels. However, the reality of using the telephone is that the tone of your voice becomes your primary effective communication channel. It actually replaces sight as the primary sense and becomes as much as 85% of the message you are trying to convey (**Figure 22**).

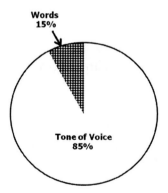

Figure 22: Words and Tone of Voice

Your task in using the telephone as a means of communicating your sales message is to find a way in which to replace the missing visual medium.

Quite often, it is more important how we say things, rather than what we say. In **Figure 22**, you can see that tone of voice is nearly six times more important than the words used. Say aloud and record yourself saying the following sentence which is repeated seven times, placing the emphasis on the underlined words or words:

1. **I** DID NOT SAY YOU STOLE HER PURSE.
2. I **DID NOT** SAY YOU STOLE HER PURSE.
3. I DID NOT **SAY** YOU STOLE HER PURSE.
4. I DID NOT SAY **YOU** STOLE HER PURSE.
5. I DID NOT SAY YOU **STOLE** HER PURSE.
6. I DID NOT SAY YOU STOLE **HER** PURSE.
7. I DID NOT SAY YOU STOLE HER **PURSE.**

Each time you change the emphasis onto a different word, the meaning of the sentence also changes. So even though two people say the same things, they can be perceived to have said different things. The tone of your voice can tell other people how sincere you are; whether they should believe you are honest; your level of confidence; if you are bored; upset; interested in them – and in addition, how you stress certain words will increase or decrease their importance. Learning to add pitch adds emphasis to your message as opposed to using a monotone, which will bore the receiver.

Say aloud "Thank you very much" without emphasising any of the words. Now repeat it, with particular emphasis on the word 'very'. Do you notice the difference? How did you place the emphasis on the word 'very'? Try it again this time by lowering the tone of your voice when you say 'very'. Immediately after, say the sentence again, but this time when you come to the word 'very', raise your voice. Again, you should be able to notice quite a significant difference. By raising your voice at the appropriate moment, it places a greater positive emphasis on a word, and more important on the perceived sincerity of the word. Now try saying it again, this time while turning the corners of your mouth down, as though you are sad. Now repeat the exercise whilst smiling. It is certain that the sentence that sounds the most positive is the one said whilst smiling, and that is a very important lesson. Remember the phrase: 'smile while you dial' – it can make a dramatic difference to the call.

Words to avoid

As words and tone are all you have when using the telephone, it is worth taking note of some words that I have found either can be misconstrued, or prospects and customers can react negatively to:

- **But:** In assertiveness training, this is said to be an aggressive word and can often be taken as challenging what the customer has said.

- **Why:** When used on its own, it too can be misconstrued as aggressive or direct, putting the customer 'on the spot'.

- **Busy:** No salesperson is ever too busy to see a prospective customer. He/she may be 'engaged elsewhere on his/her territory' or 'his/her diary may be full on that particular day'. But he/she is never 'too busy'.

- **Problem:** Similarly, salespeople never have 'problems' that prevent them from seeing a prospect. Their 'time may have to be devoted to ...' on that day or a 'prior appointment/engagement may prevent them attending at that particular time'. But 'problems' never get in the way of seeing customers.

- **Guarantee:** It can be dangerous to guarantee an appointment, delivery, visit, etc. A simple traffic jam could prevent you attending a 'guaranteed meeting'. The customer may accept your reason for being delayed but lateness against a guarantee reflects badly on your personal (and the company's) public relations image.

- **Try:** Never use the word 'try' in the wrong context. If you say, "I'll try and get there for 10.30 a.m.", it makes your contact unsure and he will assume that you will not be there on time. When making appointments, you should never book visits so close together that there is any doubt you can make each one comfortably. If you get a call asking you to visit on an already crowded day, it is better to use the word 'endeavour'. (Do not say, "I'll do my best" for the same reasons as above – the customer will assume the opposite.)

THE WAY YOU TALK

Here are some issues you may want to consider and might have to unlearn in order to help replace the visual medium when using the telephone to sell.

Talking too quickly

The more nervous you are, the faster you talk. The faster you talk, the less your customer will take in, other than to want to end the call. An acceptable rate to speak at is about 120 words per minute. Any faster will not be understood, and significantly slower can irritate people. How quickly do you speak? Read the following passage aloud in your normal speaking voice and record it as you do so:

> In face-to-face communication, the most important medium is the visual. On the telephone, you are restricted to words and how you say those words. Very few people, however, do anything about the way they sound, assuming that the way they hear their own voice in their heads is the way that other people hear it. The problem is that you get so used to the sound of your own voice that it is impossible to be truly objective about the way it sounds. What does your voice sound like to other people? Have you ever recorded it? Probably. And what did you say upon first hearing a recording of your voice? That's right. "That doesn't sound like me". And yet obviously it was. You see, if you were to give a recording of your voice to someone else and ask him or her who they thought it was, they would have no difficulty in identifying you. The voice you hear inside your head is not the voice other people hear. You hear your voice from inside your skull. Others hear your voice through their ears. The two results can be dramatically different. The amazing thing is that 95% of salespeople NEVER record their voice and listen to it, which could be the first vital step in improving the delivery of their message.

When you play the recording back, stop the recording after one minute. You should have reached the section 'And what did you say upon first hearing a recording of your voice? That's right. "That doesn't sound like me"'.

Try reading the passage again from the table below, with a watch handy, attempting to read 20 words every 10 seconds. Record yourself until you get it about right.

Message	Time
In face-to-face communication, the most important medium is the visual. On the telephone, you are restricted to words	10
and how you say those words. Very few people, however, do anything about the way they sound, assuming that the	20
way they hear their own voice in their heads is the way that other people also hear it. The problem is	30
that you get so used to the sound of your own voice that it is impossible to be truly objective	40
about the way it sounds. What does your voice sound like to other people? Have you ever recorded it? Probably.	50
And what did you say upon first hearing a recording of your voice? That's right. "That doesn't sound like me".	60
And yet obviously it was. You see, if you were to give a recording of your voice to someone else	70
and ask them who they thought it was, they would have no difficulty in identifying you. The voice you hear	80
inside your head is not the voice other people hear. You hear your voice from inside your skull. Other people	90
hear your voice through their ears. The two results can be dramatically different. The amazing thing is that 95% of salespeople	100
NEVER record their voice and listen to it, which could be the first vital step in improving the delivery of their message.	112

Table 2: Reading a Sales Message

The more you practice this, the more ingrained in your style of delivery it will become.

Sit up straight or stand up

If you have to sit down, sit up straight. It helps you to breathe better. Better still, if you want to take control, stand up. When you sit down to use the telephone, and your papers are on your desk, the natural body posture is a hunched back and a concave chest. This will restrict your breathing, and all it takes is a few negative calls for you to sink further into your chair. Within a short space of time, your voice will sound lack-lustre and boring. Standing up will make your voice sound more dynamic and positive.

Avoid jargon

The biggest problem is that you probably do not even know you use it. It is also highly probable that your colleagues use the same jargon and therefore the chances are that if you ask them to listen to you, they will miss the jargon words you use as well. The best way to find out if you are using jargon is to record what you say, and ask someone at home to listen to you. It also could be fun!

Be clear in your speech

The English language is full of words that sound the same but mean something different, for example:

- Accept, except.
- Access, excess.
- Addition, edition.
- Affect, effect.
- Assistants, assistance.
- Cite, site, sight.
- Council, counsel.
- It's, its.
- Loose, lose.
- Passed, past.
- Personal, personnel.
- Principal, principle.
- Stationary, stationery.

- There, Their, They're.
- To, too, two.
- Whose, who's.
- Your, you're.

You can probably think of a lot more. It is important for you to practice and distinguish between letters such as 'F' and 'S', between 'D' and 'T', 'P' and 'B', and between 'N' and 'M'. Speak clearly and not too fast. You do not have to change your accent, just perhaps the clarity of what you say.

Diction

It is very easy on the telephone to mishear what it is someone else says, even if you ask him or her to spell something out. You may have heard the police or air traffic controllers use a system of identifying letters using what is called the Phonetic Alphabet. For example they might say 'A' for 'Alpha' or 'F' for 'Foxtrot'. See how many you know by filling in the missing words:

A = ALPHA	B =	C =
D = DELTA	E =	F = FOXTROT
G =	H =	I =
J =	J =	L =
M =	N =	O =
P =	Q =	R =
S =	T =	U =
V =	W =	X =
Y =	Z =	

Table 3: The Phonetic Alphabet

You will find the answers in Wikipedia.[38]

---

[38] http://en.wikipedia.org/wiki/NATO_phonetic_alphabet

Using benefit statements

Whether making outgoing calls or taking incoming calls, there is very little time for you to make an impression on the telephone, so if you want to catch the customer's attention then you had better have a few benefit statements to hand. There are really only four major benefits that the customer might be interested in:

- Making money.
- Saving money.
- Saving time.
- Reducing effort.

Your task should be to script and rehearse at least one benefit statement in each of these areas – for example:

- **Making money:** "Since using our services, customers like you have increased their turnover".
- **Saving money:** "Since using our service, customers like you have reduced their costs".
- **Saving time:** "Since using our services, customers like you have found they have more time to concentrate on the important things in their businesses".
- **Reducing effort:** "Since using our service, customers like you appear to find the effort to operate is less".

WHEN IS THE BEST TIME TO CALL?

Contacting people at the wrong time can get you off to a bad start. You need to think long and hard about the best time for telephoning. Your company may have conducted some research already, but if not then it is a good idea for you to collate and develop your own database of best and worst times to call people, dividing contacts into categories. Although it can be difficult to gauge exactly when is the best time, common-sense suggests avoiding the following times:

- **Private individuals:** Before 9 a.m. and between 5.30 and 7.00 p.m. Think about the busy times in your own home.

- **Senior managers:** After 10 a.m. By this time, they are usually well into the swing of meetings for the day.
- **Shops:** Before 10 a.m. and between 12.00 and 3.00 p.m. Buyers are usually tied up before the shop opens and short-staffed during the lunch breaks.

Some of the best times to telephone are:

- **Private individuals:** Weekends – but avoid before 10 a.m., late afternoons and Monday morning – when people take time off it is usually tagged onto a weekend. Be careful about the local culture.
- **Senior managers or the self-employed:** Before 8.45 a.m. and after 5.30 p.m. – they have a tendency to answer the telephone themselves then.

THERE IS A TIME TO QUIT

In my experience, some people initially do not want an appointment, but, if you go on long enough, will capitulate. When you call on them, however, they are either out, or meeting them turns out to be a complete waste of time. You need to be able to gauge when enough is enough. My rule of thumb is that if a person refuses three times, it is usually time to call it a day. That is not to say that you cannot still make a sale – for example, you might say "Obviously it appears that I was not able to convince you of the benefit of our services this time. However, we are always bringing out new lines and products. Would it be all right with you if I called you again when that happens?"

In addition, although you might not have sold an appointment to the customer this time, that does not stop them introducing you to someone who might – for example, "Obviously, it appears that I was not able to convince you of the benefit of our services this time. However, whenever I've spoken to someone like you, it usually turns out that they know of someone else who might benefit from our services. Would that be the case with you?"

NEXT ...

- Ask yourself, "How would I want to be dealt with on the telephone?"
- Make a habit of recording your end of telephone conversations so that you can review the effectiveness of your communication skills.
- Role-play often.

CHAPTER 8
USING VISUAL COMMUNICATION TO SELL YOURSELF

SUMMARY

- First impressions count.
- You do not get a second chance to sell yourself the first time.
- A picture says a thousand words.

FIRST IMPRESSIONS

It may be unfortunate, but first impressions count: we all make decisions about other people within a couple of minutes of meeting them. It then can take a lifetime for us to change our views of them. You probably do not have a lifetime to convince the customer.

There must have been a time when you walked into a shop, or a restaurant, or even someone's house where your first instinct was to say to yourself, "I don't want to be here". If you want to turn more of your customers into buyers, you have to ask yourself, "What will the customer expect to see when you turn up to see them?" Most customers are looking for a professional salesperson to deal with them. Here are some tips:

- You need to think about the way you look and dress: It may be better to dress down than to dress up.
- Think about the customer: Wearing obviously expensive clothes might not be appropriate if your customers are generally short of money; they might think twice about who is making money from the sale.

- Similarly, wearing jeans and a T-shirt would not be appropriate if you are selling to the Head Buyer of a department store.
- If you are overweight, then wear clothes that help to tone the weight down by choosing dark colours; similarly, longer hair accentuates weight.
- Your hair should be clean and well-groomed: Before you go in to see a customer, comb your hair.
- Avoid wearing distinctive or noticeable jewellery: Keep your expensive watch for the weekends.
- The equipment and sales aids you bring with you should be clean: It is pointless trying to convince a customer about the quality of your goods and services if the material you bring with you has seen much better days.

VISUALS AND WORD PICTURES

It is said that a picture paints a thousand words. Interflora got it right with its catchphrase, "Say it with flowers". People believe what they see. Most people believe what they see on television. Many people believe what they read in the newspapers. Most people believe what they see on a computer screen. If you cannot demonstrate your product, either because it is too big, complicated, or intangible, but you want your sales presentation to make a convincing impact, you should use visuals to support your presentation. Visuals also help the customer to remember your presentation. In general terms, if we accept that people have been conditioned to believe what they see, and question what they hear, then perhaps it could be a good idea to translate a lot of the things we want to say into things that the customer can see. If you use them, be sure that the quality of any visuals you use are first class. They do not necessarily need to be expensive but they should not look cheap either.

Drawing diagrams
If, for some reason, either you or your company you cannot afford to buy good quality visual aids, then you can still make your sales presentation come to life by using a blank sheet of paper, and a

marker pen. Some of the best presentations I have seen have been made by salespeople drawing simple diagrams on blank paper. Use white paper and a deep colour marker pen, preferably black or dark blue. Other colours sometimes have adverse effects on some people, so you are better off sticking to black or blue. Keep any drawings you make simple. Stick to easy-to-draw shapes, such as circles, squares and triangles. Practice drawing until they look recognisable and not amateurish. Use a marker pen which has a broad surface so that your drawing can be seen from a distance.

If you can show your customer some pictures, then you are managing to compete with the way in most people receive information – from the television and the internet, using coloured pictures. It is a quicker way of getting your point across as well.

Using bullet points

If you find that your product is definitely unable to convert to a picture, then try and get the main selling points of your presentation down to a list of single-word bullet points. Then place each of these words on a separate piece of white paper. Keep practising until the way in which you write the word looks reasonably professional. Then you can start to experiment with drawing a circle around the word, or a box, or triangle. Keep working on it until the simple drawing looks effective. You will be surprised how effective it becomes in a sales presentation to be able to take out a blank sheet of paper, write a word down and draw a circle around it in order to emphasise a sales point.

Using visual imagery

Sometimes, you do not even have to use pictures. I particularly recall meeting a remarkable saleswoman who used visual imagery in the sale. I was buying a newspaper in a newsagent shop. If you pay attention, you often see salespeople making presentations. I love to eavesdrop. There is always something new you can learn. The saleswoman obviously worked for Slush Puppie,[39] a company that makes iced drinks from a machine. What she did was to take a piece

---

[39] http://en.wikipedia.org/wiki/Slush_Puppie

of paper out of her case, which she unfolded until it was four feet square. She held it up in front of the shop manager and said: "Mr Harris, if I was to say to you that this piece of paper could be worth €20,000 a year to you, would you be interested finding out more?" Only a fool would say "No" – and Mr Harris was no fool. She then placed the piece of paper on the floor, and said: "If you let me put one of our machines on top of this piece of paper and it does not improve your turnover by €20,000 in 12 months, I will personally take it away, and you can keep the piece of paper for nothing". The manager and I both laughed out loud. It was one of the shortest, most succinct, and best sales presentations I had witnessed in ages. The two outcomes of that presentation were that a) she made the sale, and b) I hired her to work for me. Unfortunately for me, she got even better at selling, and within six months, was running her own successful company.

INFLUENCERS IN COMMUNICATION

The main influencers in communication when we meet customers divide into body language (what people see), and what people hear (the words we use and how we speak). Of these, body language (non-verbal communication) is the most important (**Figure 23**).

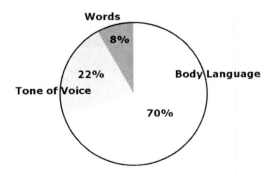

Figure 23: The Importance of Body Language

It is said that body language represents up to 70% of our communication with others. The words we use count for only around 8%, and our tone of voice 22%.

Body language

We know that people read more into how things are being said than into what is being said. If someone says one thing, and shows non-verbally that they actually mean or believe something else, then we will respond to the non-verbal signals rather than the verbal signals. Where the words and the body language match, this is known as congruence; where they do not, this is incongruence.

If the words you use have a positive content, but the body language you display is negative, then the customer will feel that you possibly are being dishonest. If the words and body language are closed – both negative – then your chances of success are zero. You might say that no salesperson, and certainly not you, would be so stupid as to deliver negative messages, but it happens a lot. Without practice, and most importantly, without feedback, most people harbour, and display, some form of negative tendencies, in both/either the words they use and/or the non-verbal signals they display. More often than not, negative words can be used in combination with positive body language. Sometimes this works, but sometimes it can be seen as being mischievous. It depends on the customer, but it is not worth the risk, unless you know the customer very well. The only form of professional sales communication is open, where the words used, and the body language displayed, are both positive.

Customers' body language

One of the strongest reasons for having a scripted opening to your sales presentation is so that you can deliver your opening on automatic pilot whilst you observe the customer's body language. The more often you use a series of prepared sales statements, the more often you can take notice of whether the words and body language used by the customer are congruent are not. If not, then you should check it out.

Examples of negative customer body language include:

- Their arms are folded across their chest.
- They have their legs tucked beneath the chair they are sitting on with their knees together.

- They sit back, and lean away from you.
- They move back.
- Their face is expressionless.
- They appear tense.
- If they are standing, they might have their hands clasped behind their back, or their arms folded.
- Their handshake is likely to be limp, and they withdraw it quickly.
- They do not make eye contact.

Examples of positive customer body language include:

- Their arms are open.
- If sitting, their legs are in front and knees apart.
- They lean forward towards you.
- They move closer.
- They smile.
- If standing, their legs are apart.
- They use hand movements to express themselves.
- Their handshake is firm.
- They make regular eye contact.

Mirror, pace, lead

Although there is much about NLP that leaves me cold, I do agree that a bond can be established between you and the customer by being a) aware of the non-verbal signals that they are displaying, and b) matching your behaviour, as appropriate. There is a limit, however, and if you use this technique you need to be extremely well practised; otherwise, inevitably, you will be found out.

Before NLP, this process was called 'Mirror, Pace and Lead'. The theory is that if you mirror the body talk of people around you, especially their hand movements and the way in which they move their head, and make eye contact, that person will feel that you already know them, and they will be more receptive to your ideas or points. Pacing means that not only do you mirror their gestures, but also their breathing rate. Consequently, as you both become synchronised, they will feel an even deeper rapport with you. Leading means that once you have established rapport with the other person, you can get them to alter their body language, by gradually altering your own body language.

POSITIONING

Where you stand or sit in relation to the customer is important: this becomes the arena in which you play. As with any team, you tend to feel more comfortable at home than away. The customer's workplace/office may be seen as an away game, but that does not mean that you have to accept the way in which the pitch has been laid out. If you look at **Figure 24**, which shows the potential seating positions of a customer and a salesperson, then the least co-operative seating positions are A and B, the most co-operative seating position is C, followed by D. A lot of salespeople end up sitting in position A, and when I questioned this, they said that it is the customer's office or premises, and generally that is where they are shown to sit.

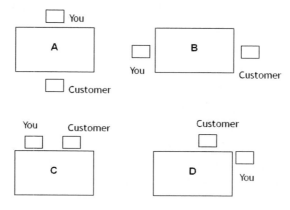

Figure 24: Positioning I: Potential Seating Positions

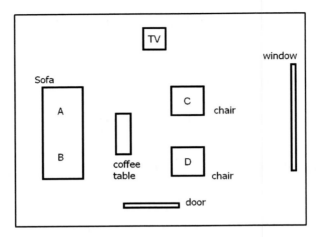

Figure 25: Positioning II: Visiting Customers at Their Home

The same sort of thing happens with salespeople who visit customers at home (**Figure 25**). The chances are that most will be shown a seat opposite wherever the customer is sitting. If there is only one customer, then the most co-operative seating position is either A or B, provided that the customer also is sitting on the sofa. However, this does not cater for our reluctance, salespeople and customers, to be too near to each other. Once again, the excuse is usually "That's where the customer asked me to sit".

In shops, showrooms, warehouses and factories, the story is the same: salespeople often are uncomfortable with the way in which the sales space has been organised. Being uncomfortable makes you look uncomfortable, and some of this discomfort will be read by the customer either as a lack of confidence or as dishonesty. The excuse is always "it's not my space". Yet even when we visit salespeople in their own space, the same basic mistakes are made.

Take control

The reason why this happens is that the customer is in control. Successful salespeople take control of the situation and the environment instead, but create a feeling for the customer where they believe that they are really in control. In reality, wherever the customer sits in their own office or in their home, it still remains their space. They would be comfortable lying on the floor, hanging from the ceiling, or sprawled out on the desk or table. We make too many assumptions about what we think customers will and will not tolerate in terms of our asking to sit in a particular place at a table, desk or showcase.

In **Figure 25**, there really is no ideal place to sit. Sofas and armchairs are made specifically to relax in. If you are making sales presentations, it might be useful for the customer to stay awake. In addition, the worst place to be in a customer's home is in front of the television. Some salespeople ask the customer to switch the television off. The point is that you need to take charge of the selling space. It is up to you to dictate where and how your sales presentation will be conducted. The sales space needs to be positioned in such a way that it will give you the greatest opportunity to show the client what your goods and services are.

Showing the customer a visual
Taking visuals aids to show a customer gives you the opportunity to arrange the seating in the most conducive way for a professional sales interview. Every salesperson should have a set of visuals to show customers. Then it is simply a matter of organising the seating to best advantage – as shown in **Figure 26**.

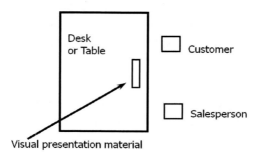

Figure 26: Positioning III: Showing the Customer a Visual

The purpose should always be to create a 'V' shape (**Figure 27**) where the focus of the sale is the visual. The salesperson acts as facilitator. In this way, the customer feels more in control, and is less threatened by the sales process.

Figure 27: Positioning IV: Focusing the Sale

This is how most people receive information. By sitting in front of a visual, and listening to a facilitator (a television, or the internet). The only issue is how to get the customer to agree either to move from behind their desk to sit beside you, or away from the lounge to the dining room table. I have heard many salespeople say to me, "I can't do that. Customers would object". The fact is that they do not, and they will not. By taking charge and saying to the customer, "I have a couple of items I'd like to show you. It helps to keep me on track, and most of my existing customers find it easier to understand if I use these visuals. To do that, I need to sit at a desk/table. Would it be better to sit at the kitchen table or the dining room table?" Alternatively, in the case of an office, "I have a couple of items I'd like to show you. It helps to keep me on track and most of my existing customers find it easier to understand if I use these visuals. To show them to your best advantage, we need to sit at the same side of the desk. Can I sit here?" The customer always says "Yes".

Unrealistic expectations
A word of warning: people often have expectations of body language that are unrealistic, thinking that they will be able to read people's minds by learning what gestures and mannerisms mean. There are a number of books and training films on the subject that go to great pains to tell the reader or viewer that it is very difficult to say that

specific gestures or mannerisms have specific meanings; that it is important to read the gesture in the context of the whole picture – to look for the 'cluster of gestures' before interpreting meaning – however, these same books go on to tell you what the gestures mean!

For example, rubbing your nose means you are about to deceive the person to whom you are talking, pulling your ear when you are listening means you are being negative or switched-off to what you are hearing – or either could just be an itch. The fact is that you simply cannot read people's thoughts from the gestures they are making, and this is borne out by research carried out by Mehrabian, Williams[40] and others. Reading individual gestures is similar to taking a single word out of an entire paragraph, and saying that you can tell what that entire paragraph is about by knowing that one single word. What we can do is read the paragraph and then, by reading their body talk, we can gain a sense of the other person's feelings or attitudes.

Body language is a specialist subject, and this section aims merely to provide the reader with a basic understanding of the subject, but enough to be able to put it to good use.

NEXT ...

- Convert the main elements of your sales presentation into word pictures.

- Invest in the best possible visuals you can afford to gain customer attention.

- Stay in control when you are using visuals – your verbal message is also important.

---

[40] Mehrabian, A. and Williams, M. (1969). 'Non-verbal concomitants of perceived and intended persuasiveness', *Journal of Personality and Social Psychology*, Vol. 13, No.1.

CHAPTER 9
WHAT MAKES PEOPLE BUY?

SUMMARY

- Most people do not like being sold to. By recognising this fact alone, successful salespeople aim to put the buyer in charge of the sales process.
- This does not mean abdicating your personal selling responsibilities by simply saying "Tell me what you want, and I'll give it to you at whatever price you want to pay for it".
- By structuring your sales process in such a way that the buyer feels in control of the sales process, you will achieve the same aims as though they were actually in control.
- Sometimes selling is about perceptions, not reality.

There is no proven formula to explain the motives behind consumer behaviour. The reasons for purchasing certain goods vary between individuals. Some people buy goods merely for what the goods signify about them to others, and not in terms of their functionality. A prime example is clothing. Society appears to be pervaded by designer labels. In many circles, it is considered far more distinguished to wear a Calvin Klein suit rather than a practically identical own label garment from a local department store. Some commentators argue that functionality in society has completely vanished: instead, we consume only what we are sold by advertising and peer pressure.

This may be relevant to you as a salesperson, and some have argued that you need to analyse consumer behaviour in order to be successful. To do this, it has been proposed that you should consider carefully all the factors that may drive a certain type of person to buy a particular product. You are asked to bear in mind that the consumer begins the buying process with a specific mind-set – in other words, society has moulded them into a particular way of thinking, and they already have a number of pre-conceived ideas about the product they might buy. Influences on the consumer may include factors such as:

- Cultural background.
- Peer pressure.
- Impulse buying.

In a sense, cultural background is implicit to the buying process as culture is something that we learn – we are not born with ideologies. The influence of our families, friends and colleagues shape us into a certain 'reference group', in which similar trends of behaviour can be found. Therefore, advertisers frequently gear their campaigns to target these particular groups, as to do so is an infinitely lucrative process. An example of this is sports clothing, in particular soccer shirts. Manufacturers now design the shirts of soccer clubs to suit the everyday fashion sense of the fans, rather than the functionality of the shirt on the pitch.

How we are viewed by others often is very important to us, and so we may wish to change our image. Manufacturers can tap into this by telling that person is that if they buy a certain product, it will allow them to become the person they aspire to be.

BUYING MOTIVES

In *Creative Selling Today*,[41] Stan Kossen talks about Maslow's[42] Hierarchy of Needs (**Figure 28**), which categorises human needs as:

- Basic physical needs.
- Safety and security needs.
- Social needs.

---

[41]   Kossen, S. (1982). *Creative Selling Today*, New York: Harper & Row.
[42]   Maslow, A.H. (1954). *Motivation and Personality*, New York: Harper & Row.

- Self-esteem, self-respect and status needs.
- Self-realisation needs – the need for feelings of accomplishment.

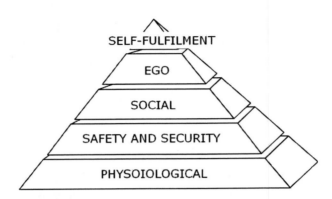

Figure 28: Maslow's Hierarchy of Needs

He says that, if salespeople recognise these needs in the consumer, then they can be an invaluable tool in analysing the habits of the buyer. Subsequently, the salesperson can gear their approach towards a specific need.

If you re-kindle a particular need within a customer, you may be able to persuade them to purchase your product. Analysing their needs can be beneficial in doing this, and you would need to consider:

- Any hobbies/leisure interests they may have.
- The reasons why the goods you are selling could be pleasing to them.
- How your goods can render them a particular service.
- Ways in which your goods could make their lives less stressful.
- The *raison d'être* of your prospect, which could be anything that really gets them motivated.[43]

Similar to the way in which salespeople have goals, consumers also have goals. Consumers buy in order to attain the belief that they will

---

[43]   Auer, J.T. (1991). *Inspired Selling,* London: Kogan Page.

have a prosperous life. Their ideals of a good life are based on a series of binary opposites. For example, people aspire to be:

- Healthy rather than sick.
- Vivacious as opposed to dull.
- Physically fit rather than unfit.
- Well-liked rather than despised.
- Part of a group as opposed to being ostracised.
- Assured rather than vulnerable.
- Easygoing as opposed to being stressed.
- Attractive in contrast to unattractive.
- Prosperous rather than impoverished.
- Independent rather than dependent on others.

Advertising can tap into these binary opposites, and demonstrate how consumers can reach their life goals by buying specific products. These goals often symbolise status, and by achieving them, people demonstrate to others their status through the perceptions they have consumed. Examples of this include:

- Mr Doyle buys an expensive estate car for himself and his family, as he believes that it is the ultimate icon of the middle-class suburban family. Many of the other families in his neighbourhood have cars similar or inferior to this car, and colleagues from a similar background at work have recommended it to him.
- Mr Smith buys a top of the range sports car for himself, as he believes it is the ultimate status symbol for a young executive such as himself. His friends all envy his new purchase, as they believe it will make him more attractive to the opposite sex.

In this respect, consumer wants are different to consumer needs. There is conceivably no real need to consume as many of the things we buy that we do. Nevertheless, advertising often touches upon a particular want or desire within us that will motivate us to buy something on the off chance that it will make us happier.

Ideology forms an important part of buyer wants and needs, as consumers have certain beliefs about the potential effects of indulging their wants. The beliefs that have become innate to consumers through exposure to ideological institutions (family, school, work, and even the internet and social media) mean that they make assumptions, sometimes even unconsciously, when coming to buy a product. For example, people assume that a personal computer or mobile telephone is good because it has a recognised logo on it, in complete ignorance of the fact that a cheaper model by an unknown manufacturer may be superior in terms of performance. Therefore, salespeople often are involved in a process of selling an idea of quality, not actually quality itself.[44]

BUYING OR SELLING

There is a saying, "If you don't let the customer buy, then you'll have to sell to them". Would you rather sell to people, or have them buy from you? The fact is most of us do not like being sold to. If someone shows an interest in something that you have, your response can be significantly different depending upon whether they say, "Where did you buy that?" or "Who sold you that?" We like to feel that we make decisions about what we do, not that someone has made the decisions on our behalf or even tricked us into buying something.

In a survey of customer buying behaviour, 50% of customers questioned about consumer durables had turned to friends and relations for information to support their buying decision.[45] In the same way, they make decisions not to buy based on the bad experience of others. Williams[46] said that "word-of-mouth research conducted in the United States has found that bad product or service experience is relayed to twice as many people as good, and when asked which sources of information they trusted when considering a purchase, consumers put fellow consumers at the top of the list". She goes on to say that:

[44] O'Shaughnessy, J. (1987). *Why People Buy*, Oxford: Oxford University Press.
[45] Howard, J.A. and Sheth, J.N. (1969). *Theory of Buyer Behaviour*, Hoboken, NJ: John Wiley & Sons Ltd.
[46] Perception or reality? M. Williams. Managing Service Quality. May. 1993

... preventing people from telling others of bad service experience by successfully handling complaints on the spot is a well-recognised and highly-useful way of reducing the number of negative comments about service performance that get into circulation, thus leaving the good points looking better.

Personal sources are the single most important source affecting decisions. Annual research into the buying habits of consumers in financial services[47] shows that more people seek advice about finance from friends and relatives than from financial advisers. This tells us that people do not like to be sold to. They like to feel that they are making buying decisions. I call it 'the motivation to buy'.

How to motivate the buyer
We always feel better when we are in control of the buying process. Imagine that you have made a presentation to the customer about your product. Perhaps your product is complicated. You are considered to be the expert. You have made your presentation, and you have advised your customer that buying this product would be a good choice. They agree, and complete the order. How do you feel? Without doubt, deservedly pleased. You also could say that you feel a sense of achievement and recognition. A sense of achievement that you have made a sale and a feeling of recognition in that the customer has recognised you as being someone to transact business with. Insofar as Maslow's Hierarchy of Human Needs is concerned, you will be motivated at the highest levels.

In this same vignette, and thinking about Maslow's Hierarchy, at which level would you consider that the customer's motivation is operating? Perhaps physiological, safety and security, or even at a social needs level. Our research shows that when customers are sold to, they never experience satisfaction of either Ego Needs (recognition), or Self-Fulfilment Needs (a sense of achievement). Why? Because the salesperson has kept the high ground for themselves, and left the customer to more basic needs' satisfaction. In this way, the customer learns that dealing with this particular

---

[47]   Mintel.

salesperson is emotionally unrewarding, and is not inclined to either return to that salesperson, or to recommend that salesperson to their own friends and acquaintances.

People buy emotionally not logically

Only 10% of a buyer's decision to purchase is based on logic and facts, and 90% on emotional reaction. People buy what they want, and not necessarily what they need. If that matches up with what they need, then well and good. If it does not match what they need, but it is still what they want, then that is good too. It is the customer who needs to make the final choice. Whether they take your advice is a matter for them. Remember that true customer satisfaction comes from individuals making their own mind up, and gaining a sense of achievement from having done so.

Further evidence to support the premise that people buy for emotional rather than logical reasons was provided through a survey published in the *US News and World Report* by the Rockefeller Corporation of Pittsburgh, where the following facts emerged on why customers stop buying from their regular suppliers:

- 1% died.
- 3% moved away.
- 5% formed other friendships.
- 9% for competitive reasons.
- 14% due to product dissatisfaction.
- 68% quit because of an attitude of indifference toward the customer, by one or more persons representing the supplier.

Whilst some research suggests that buyers in companies are mostly concerned with price, and terms and conditions, for the service provided,[48] the overwhelming evidence points to the fact that people buy, or do not buy, based on emotion.

[48] Hayes, H.M. and Hartley, S.W. (1989). 'How buyers view industrial salespeople', *Industrial Marketing Management*, May, pp.73-80.

Finding out is better than being told

One of the greatest American sales trainers is Tom Hopkins. When he was on tour in the UK, I attended one of his inspirational seminars. He said that one of the keys to understanding customer thinking is that customers believe that 'if the customer says it, then it must be true. If the salesman says it, then it's probably just sales talk'. That is a terrific lesson to learn and is worth repeating: 'If the customer says it, then it must be true. If the salesman says it, then it's probably just sales talk'. The task for you is to get the customer to make the running, for the customer to make the buying decision.

Recognise also that we do not particularly like to make decisions. There is always the feeling that the decision might be wrong. For that reason, a lot of people may be put off the decision to buy, either to think it over, or to check it out with another person. This is especially so if the impetus for buying was instigated by the salesperson in the first place.

If you want to avoid this behaviour, then you have to put the customer in charge of the decision-making process. What do we need to make a decision? Information. In what format? In a format that we can understand. How is most product information provided? Jargon – or at the very least, in the sort of format that most people find it difficult to absorb, which in turn makes decision-making difficult.

Relationships between buyers and sellers

In addition to the motivational factors covered so far, you also should be aware that buyers are no different to the mass of the population. Their buying choices are mostly affected by emotional reasons. This can even come down to whether they like you or not. Chesnut and Jacoby[49] argue that, when it comes down to the customer deciding whether to purchase from a range of similar products, the decision can be heavily influenced by the salesperson's attractiveness. Unfortunately, it is a fact of life that attractive people receive a better initial hearing than unattractive people. Fortunately, beauty is only skin deep. If the messages coming from the salesperson do not match

---

[49] Chesnut, R.W. and Jacoby, J. (1984). *The Impact of Interpersonal Attraction on Salesperson Effectiveness*, Lanham, MD: Lexington Books.

the initial perception that the customer has of the seller, then a sale will not necessarily ensure. It is also a fact that attractiveness encompasses more than just looks. It is about the way in which we present ourselves, including all facets of communication.

THE COMPETITION AND PRICE RESISTANCE

You ought to know whether your product or service is expensive or not compared to the competition, and whether the reason for the price differential with the competition is justifiable. The price of your product should never be considered in isolation. In order to make a decision about whether to buy or not, the customer generally attempts to compare your product to a competitor, based on:

- The competition's price.
- Your personal image.
- Your company's image.
- The satisfaction of their logical needs.
- The satisfaction of their emotional needs.
- Particular and general benefits.
- The product's purported reliability and durability.
- Any potential purchase risks.

So unless your customer is made aware of all these factors, he or she will not be in a position to make a judgement based on value, but only on price. Therefore the golden rule is 'don't sell the price until you've sold the product'.

Ideally, and following a full product presentation, your customer should say, "Yes, that seems to be what we need. Now, what does it cost?" That is your cue to sell the price and the sale terms. However, some customers may still hesitate and need your help to overcome a resistance, not always to the price itself but to the idea of committing financial resources that are already committed, to a product where resources are not yet committed, and therefore may represent a risk. The following ideas may help you to overcome your customers' price resistance:

- **Reduce the price to its lowest common denominator:** A price can usually be expressed in terms of cost per person, square foot, shelf, hour or minutes, packet, weight, individual item, page, etc.

- **Compare the price to expected savings:** Express the customer's needs in financial loss terms, and compare these to the expected savings with your product in place – for example, current loss per hour (€35) less product costs per hour (€23) = saving per hour (€12).

- **Compare the price to everyday expenses:** For example, the price is equivalent to: four peak-time business telephone calls, one gallon of petrol, a box of photocopier paper, membership of a motoring organisation, a paperback book, etc.

At some stage, you may be faced with dealing with a customer who is currently supplied by a competitor selling a similar product or service to your own. Unless the customer has asked to see you, you should assume that they are satisfied with their current supplier. The reason for this assumption is to avoid criticism of their current supplier by you. If anyone is to criticise their current supplier, then that should be the customer's role, and even if they do so to you, you should not join in.

So how do you find out whether they are satisfied with their current supplier? The worst thing you can do is to ask, "Are you satisfied with your current supplier?" The odds are very high that they will say "Yes", even if they are not.

From your own perspective, you already know that probably not everything your company does is sweetness and light. All sorts of things can go wrong, such as:

- Late delivery.
- Out of stock.
- Mistakes from order to delivery.
- Damaged goods.
- The customer could find out later that they could have bought cheaper elsewhere.

The only thing you can do is, once again, to develop a story that a) sounds believable and b) puts the onus on the customer to tell you in what circumstances they would change supplier – for example, "Mr Doyle, I will make an assumption here that you are satisfied with your current supplier. Would that be the case?" If they say "No", then the sale is yours to lose. If they say "Yes", you could then say "Could you tell me, Mr Doyle, what is there about your present supplier that keeps you as a customer?" It is pointless offering to match what the competition offers without offering something extra. The only reason why thousands of people constantly change telephone and energy suppliers is to get cheaper telephone or energy charges. You have to find out what it would take for them to change – for example, "Just so that I know, Mr Doyle, what would it take for you to even consider changing suppliers?"

If they tell you, it is not a simple matter of promising to deliver that very thing. Many customers want to be loyal to a good supplier, provided they feel that they are receiving good service and value for money. Most, however, might consider a compromise – for example, "Mr Doyle. I would be very lucky if you decided to change your current supplier without giving it some thought. What I would like to propose is that, in order to help you decide, you let me supply you with a small percentage of your usual order so that you can sample first-hand the sort of service we provide". Most reasonable customers will meet your compromise. After that, it is up to you to prove yourself by delivering what you promise in every respect.

NEXT ...

- Ask yourself often, "What would make you buy from you?"
- What have you bought recently as a result of an emotional buying decision rather than a decision based upon need and value for money? What have you learned from this?
- How can you give buyers a sense of achievement, or recognition, in a sales situation?

CHAPTER 10

PLANNING FOR SALES SUCCESS

SUMMARY

- Planning needs to be a holistic activity, encompassing your own personal plans with that of the organisation. It is no good planning a career when the execution of your plan does not meet the company's aims and objectives.

- Those who succeed in sales keep an eye on the quality of their activity, not just the activity itself.

- Small improvements in ratios have a significant and positive effect on the bigger picture.

- You need to know in detail how you are spending your time in order to allocate that time more effectively.

A plan is only ever an ideal. Ideals are nice to have but sometimes they have to be changed. There is a danger, therefore, that you might consider planning a waste of time – given that things are constantly changing. Many salespeople are so busy trying to make a sale at every opportunity that they give the impression that planning is, if not a waste of time, a luxury they have no time for. Planning is meant to give you the best chance to achieve your objectives by forcing you to think about where it is you are going, and how you intend to get there, but it is not meant to be a straitjacket. The whole point about having a plan is to answer the question, "If you don't know where you are going, how will you know when you get there?"

Think about the last time you took a holiday. If you are like most people, you decided where to go, weighed up the cost, and compared it to what you could afford. You made various enquiries and undertook numerous discussions, before finally committing yourself to booking. Or are you one of those people who just turn up at the airport and say, "Take me anywhere?"

Planning allows you to do something that is critical to success, and that is to plan what to do when something goes wrong – to have a contingency plan and to take remedial action. There is a saying in selling that 'salespeople do not generally plan to fail, but they fail to plan'. What is certain is that a failure to plan effectively is a major contributory factor to sales failure, and could also be a prime reason for underachievement in the population at large.

Those who are successful in selling understand that, without a plan, the playing field is level between you and other salespeople. Successful salespeople understand that, without a plan, you have to rely on luck.

Some people work their plan by using the SMART system: Specific, Measurable, Achievable, Realistic, and Time-bound. You have probably encountered this in the past on a training course. Insofar as personal objectives are concerned, then this translates as follows:

- **Specific:** You should have a clear statement of what is to be achieved.
- **Measurable:** You should be able to measure whether you have achieved your objectives.
- **Achievable:** Achievement of the objectives must be physically possible.
- **Realistic:** It should be possible for anyone with your skill and talent to achieve the objective.
- **Time-bound:** You must set specific dates for achievement.

I have attended a great many courses, and read a great number of books and training manuals, all of which trot out the SMART acronym. Each part of this acronym seems the same to me. I have the feeling that whoever first thought of it, started with the name SMART, and tried to attach the descriptions to it. If it works for you, use it. If not, forget it.

TYING IN WITH THE CORPORATE PLAN

Planning sometimes is seen as an activity conducted by companies, rather than individuals. It is nevertheless important to think about the corporate planning process before putting your own personal plan together. It is no good planning a journey to the Caribbean when the organisation is putting together a plan to take the company to the Costa del Sol.

A simple view of how the corporate plan should affect your own planning process might look like that shown in **Figure 29**.

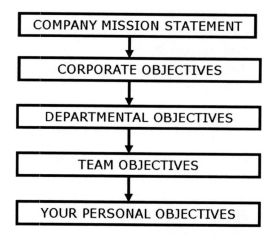

Figure 29: How the Corporate Plan Affects Your Personal Objectives

The company usually begins with a high level view of what it is in business for. You may assume that all businesses are in the business of making profit, but this is only true to a certain extent. Certainly without generating profit, businesses cannot operate, and yet there are organisational structures whose aim is not to make a profit but who still need to sell (for example, charities seeking donations, or amateur sports seeking sponsorship). Profitability and income appear at the corporate objective stage. This second stage should be pre-empted by a statement outlining the overall aims of the company. Defining corporate objectives involves the setting of high-level strategies to determine how the mission statement will be accomplished. For example, a company might use as its mission statement: "To be the best provider of vehicle service solutions for the country". Its corporate objectives then begin to explain how this would be achieved, encompassing profitability and cost control because it is from these factors that the company will determine the time scale for achievement of its company mission.

If the company wants to be the best provider of vehicle service solutions in the country, this presupposes that it wants a presence across the country. This involves premises and staff, as well as marketing and distribution activities. It also may evolve into strategies concerning capital funding and organisational status.

Following the setting of the company's corporate objectives is the process of delegating responsibilities for the achievement of parts of those objectives. This usually starts at departmental level, descending to team levels, and eventually to you.

YOUR OWN PLANS

Having acquainted yourself with the organisation's corporate plans, you now need to determine your own plans by making sure that they fit in with the bigger picture. As with the company, the first place for you to start is with your own mission statement (**Figure 30**).

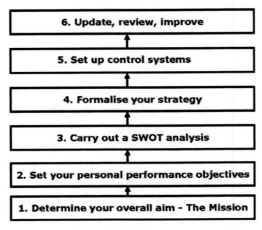

Figure 30: Personal Planning

What do you want to achieve? Your aim could be to become the best salesperson in the company. At the personal performance objectives level, you need to decide a) how this will be achieved and b) whether it fits in with the company's plans. You cannot plan to achieve personal objectives in isolation. Part of the personal planning process has to be to regularly check with your line manager so that you are in tune with what the organisation wants. If there are clear differences between the two, then you have three choices:

- Get the organisation to change its aims and objectives.

- Change your own aims and objectives.

- Leave and find more suitable employment where the company's plans and your own will match better.

A SWOT ANALYSIS

Successful people often say that, in order to plan for the future, you need a good awareness of where you are now. Many companies use the SWOT technique, which you might have come across before. SWOT stands for Strengths, Weaknesses, Opportunities, and Threats. It helps managers to focus on the things that will assist or detract them from achieving their goals. It works for individuals too. Take a blank sheet of paper and divide it up into quarters as shown in **Figure 31**.

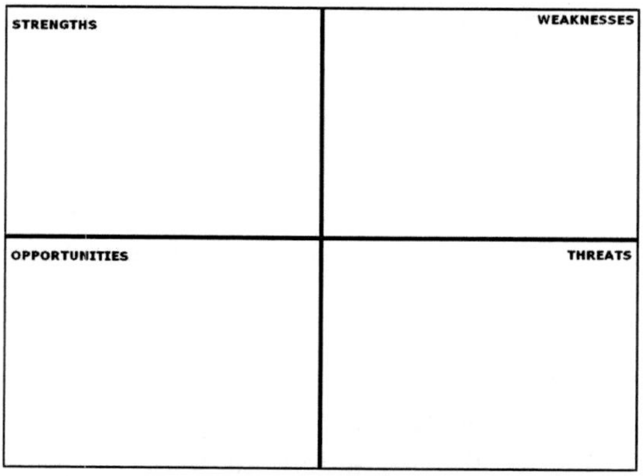

STRENGTHS	WEAKNESSES
OPPORTUNITIES	THREATS

Figure 31: SWOT Analysis

Strengths

In the first quadrant, you should list all the things that you believe might be your strengths in your sales plans. It could include the product or service itself; on the basis that whatever it is you are selling has some value for the customer. Perhaps your company has a large distribution network. It, or you, might have a well-known and respected name in the business area you are working. There may be some specific people in your company from whom you get help or who provide additional services to your customers, and who are key to your potential success.

It may be useful to write down on a separate piece of paper what particular strengths these people have. This has two benefits. It will help you when you begin to put together your sales story, and it should remind you about how strong your customer proposal is. I often find that salespeople are so focussed on their own strengths and sales proposal that they sometimes forget the benefit of having others around them. There is a third benefit. If those people you work with realise that you are singing their praises to the company's customers, it can add immeasurably to your internal working relationships.

Weaknesses

What are the weaknesses of either the company or your business proposal? Your product might be too expensive or too cheap. You could be in the wrong market for the territory you are working. Perhaps your distribution channels are not good enough compared to the competition. The procedures and processes your company employs may not be suitable for your customers. Is there an element of the service you should be providing that is missing? Look at the Opportunities section. Perhaps there are weaknesses in your potential to take advantage of opportunities as they arise. Perhaps something that you see as a strength could be seen by the customer as a weakness.

Opportunities

Given your strengths, what business opportunities do these present to you? For example, the management team of your company, or your colleagues, may have knowledge and skills that are sought after by your customers. Perhaps the fact that you have been in a certain industry sector for a number of years may allow you to promote yourself as an expert. There could be some form of Government legislation or initiative that would improve your business proposal. The general economic situation may be improving and your product could be more in demand. You might have a territorial advantage over your competitors or even your colleagues.

Threats

Are there any social, economic, or political factors that may be a threat? What is the competition doing now or planning to do? Are there any internal factors that may pose a threat to you or to your customer base? Do you rely on someone else to supply you with services or materials, without which your sales proposal would be hindered? What are your relationships like with these suppliers, and how can you ensure that the quality of service you receive from them matches the quality of service you promise your own customer?

Once you have completed this matrix, take each sector in turn and double-check that your comments are still valid in the light of your entries in the other sectors. For instance, are the elements contained under Opportunities still relevant now that you have completed the Weaknesses and Threats sections, and so on?

DEVELOPING A SALES TARGET

Based on the SWOT analysis you have carried out, you should be able to prepare sales forecasts that will show the level of sales you are likely to achieve for the period of your plan, including:

- A breakdown of your projected sales for each year, quarter, month, or week. You might even be in the sort of business where it is important to break this figure down to daily amounts.
- Your profitability to the organisation, based on income minus costs.
- Variances based on seasonal factors.
- A breakdown of the target into product groups.

Use the format in **Figure 32** as an initial target-setting guide.

	Q1	Q2	Q3	Q4
P1				
P2				
P3				
P4				

Figure 32: Target-setting for Sales Forecasts

The chart is split into the four quarters of the year and each quarter has a row for each of the three months in that quarter (Q). In addition, the chart shows four product groups (P). If you have fewer product groups, the task should be easier; if more, it simply takes longer to complete. Enter the month, the volume or units of sales you expect to make, and the value of those sales. If you are paid by results, you take a blank copy of this chart and enter the amounts you would earn from achievement of these results. Two initial things should become clear:

- Will the achievement of these results satisfy your organisation? If you work for yourself, will these results satisfy the needs that the business has?
- Will the rewards that you obtain for the achievement of these results satisfy both your own basic requirements, and the aspirations you have for yourself?

FORECASTING

The best way to forecast the future is to analyse the past. If all factors are estimated to remain the same, then looking at past performance should give you a clear indication of what future performance might be. There may be factors outside of your control, such as market changes, or people's buying habits, but you should make an effort to predict what may happen so that you can attempt to influence the level of your success.

Let us say that you are a field representative selling product X in a particular part of the country you know well. Start with a simple analysis of your results last year (see **Table 4** below).

Column A ITEM	Column B RESULTS	Column C +/- AGAINST TARGET
1. Last year's € revenue		
2. How many units did you sell?		
3. How many days did you work?		
4. How many customers bought?		
5. How many customers did you present to?		
6. How many customers did you approach?		

Table 4: Previous Year's Results

Some of this might not be relevant to your own situation. Therefore, you need to substitute what is. For example, you may not be targeted to travel a certain number of miles in a year, but you may have a budget to keep within. Therefore, at item 7 in **Table 5**, you may record how much was spent on travelling as opposed to how many miles you travelled. The important thing is to note as many measurables as you can in the ITEM column.

Column A ITEM	Column B RESULTS	Column C +/- AGAINST TARGET
1. Last year's € revenue	50,000	- 500
2. How many units did you sell?	500	+ 10
3. How many days did you work?	175	210
4. How many customers bought?	200	-
5. How many customers did you present to?	300	
6. How many customers did you approach?	500	-
7. How many miles did you drive?	30,000	-

Table 5: Current Year Results

Column B is a record of your actual achieved results. The 'actuals' that make up these items also could be referred to as 'variables', in that they are changeable and interrelated. Column C represents the variances – the difference between the target and your result.   Let us suppose that your results are shown in **Table 5**.

In this scenario, I have assumed that targets were not set for numbers of customers seen or approached, or for miles driven. I will explain why it is important to set targets for everything later but, for now, let us concentrate on the small amount of data we have. What we can now do is to analyse some data, and draw some potential conclusions about our forecast for the future. For example, by dividing item 1 by item 2, we find the average price of each unit sold, which in this case is €100. We can work out that, on average, you made €286 every working day – by dividing item 1 by item 3. Dividing item 1 by item 4 shows how much on average you made every time a customer bought from you, which in this case is €250. Dividing item 1 by item 5, we can calculate how much you made every time you made a presentation (€167) and dividing item 1 by item 6 shows how much you made every time you approached a customer (€100).

Before moving on, I would like to labour these last two points. We have said that you made €167 every time you made a presentation, and yet only 200 customers bought out of 300 presented to. Likewise, you made €100 every time you approached a customer, yet only 200 bought out of 500 approached.

Is this just semantics? No. A significant part of selling is based on attitude. Attitude, remember, is dictated by behaviour, past and present. If your behaviour is to treat each rejection as a failure, then that ultimately influences the way you behave when you meet the next prospect or customer. We are not very good at hiding our feelings and therefore, we have to create situations, or even imagine situations, that will fool ourselves into a different mindset – almost turning failure into success. It is possible to develop this data into some meaningful statistics, as shown in **Table 6**.

All that has been done here is to show some simple calculations, in technical terms called 'ratios'. You can, and should, extend this to cover as many combinations as you can initially. Later, you can decide which of these ratios you can and want to influence, but at the start, you cannot have too much data.

Column A ITEM	Column B RESULTS	Column C +/- AGAINST TARGET
1. Average € per unit	40	- 500
2. Average € per day	114	+ 10
3. Average € per customer	175	210
4. Average € per approach	67	-
5. Average miles per €	??	-
6. How many miles did you drive?	30,000	-

Table 6: Statistics Calculated from the Results

Breaking down the target

There is another effect that this process can have, more psychological than logical. Sometimes, the target can seem too big to begin. If you have ever stood at the bottom of a mountain you were about to climb, or even just a steep hill, you can understand this. It can be daunting, and many people, faced with what seems the impossible, never even begin. Clearly, in statistical terms, you can influence the level of your success by increasing any one of a number of factors. Too many salespeople and managers focus solely on activity. In this way, they eventually reach a ceiling of how many calls can be made in any 24-hour period. They also then fall into the trap of saying, "I am working as hard as I possibly can", and this might be true, but only based on making calls. There are other ways to influence success, including:

- Improving the number of approaches you make to secure an appointment.
- Improving the number of times an appointment results in a sale.
- Improving the number of appointments you make with one customer in order to make a sale.

Even small improvements in each of these areas can have a dramatic effect on your sales success.

Tracking your performance

A vital ingredient of planning, and yet most often overlooked, is in tracking where you are in comparison to where you want to be. Many tracking systems focus on numerical methods of tracking performance as can be seen in **Table 7** below.

QUARTER ONE TARGET = €12,500					
Week number	Target	Sales	Variance +/-	Cumulative +/-	Cumulative % of annual target
1	962	1,002	+40	+40	8
2	962	550	-412	-372	12
3	962	100	-862	-1,234	13
4	962	1,780	+818	-416	28
5	962	900	-62	-478	35
6	962	1,200	+238	-240	44
7	962	1,505	+543	+303	56

Table 7: Tracking Performance

Some people find this very useful; however, it can also take some time for rows of figures to sink in. Another way, and one that most people find easier to keep track of, is to plot your figures on a graph.

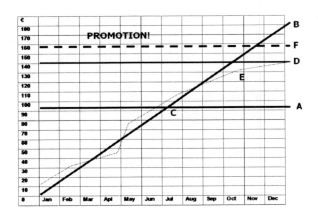

Figure 33: Graphing Performance

Figure 33 shows you the sort of graph you could construct. Line A represents your fixed costs evened out over a year. If you plot your cumulative sales (Line B), you eventually reach a point (C), which crosses line B, known as the 'break-even' point. This is where, in theory, you have paid for all of your costs (except the variable costs, etc) and are making a clear profit, either for yourself or the company.

You also could introduce other lines, parallel to line A, which could indicate what your target is, spread evenly across 12 months (D), or based on past records, divided according to past sales (E). Your company may also have a system whereby you are promoted to another level based on sales, and you could include these also (F).

RATIO ANALYSIS

A lot of salespeople find the whole subject of statistics and analysis too confusing to be bothered with, and yet all top salespeople use them. They may not call it statistical analysis, but that is what it is nevertheless. The watchword is however – simplicity. Some successful salespeople we know keep a clear and simple visual record of their success by them at all times, just to remind themselves that there is always room for improvement. As Nick Faldo says, "No one's so good they can't get better". It is an attitude all winners adopt.

Figure 34 shows the sort of ratios that many find useful, where:

- **A shows you how successful you are in contacting people:** If you continue to have a low strike rate in this area, you may be calling at the wrong times. You should record when you are making calls and what the results were. You could keep a simple record as shown above.

- **B shows your strike rate in making appointments:** You should compare it with the strike rate of your peers – especially the successful ones.

- **C shows how many times you called on your customers after making an appointment and they were not there when you turned up:** This ratio tells you how often you simply bludgeon the customer into giving you an appointment they really do not want.

If this ratio is high, you need to ask for third party help in listening into your telephone appointment-making technique.

- **D is a critical ratio – known as your strike rate:** It represents your actual success rate in front of the customer. Improving this ratio will help far more, and be less hard work, than making 50% more calls.

- **E, F, G, H, I:** If your sales process requires you to make a number of presentations in order to secure the business, then these ratios could assist you in determining where improvement is required.

- **J:** How successful are you in converting referred leads to actual sales?

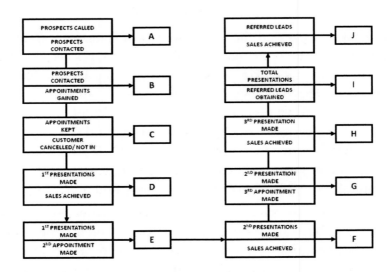

Figure 34: Ratios

NEXT ...

- Construct a personal business plan for the next 12 months' trading period.

CHAPTER 11
TIME MANAGEMENT IS ABOUT ATTITUDE, NOT SYSTEMS

SUMMARY

- You cannot stop time, buy time, borrow time, or steal time.
- Just 15 minutes a day – used differently – could change your life.
- It is not time management systems that will help you use time more effectively – it is your attitude towards the use of your time.

Some people waste time. Others try to buy time. Some people have not got any time, and others seem to have all the time in the world. For some people, time is as precious and they act as though they are on borrowed time. For others, there is always plenty of time to do things, and the later the better. When children are on holiday, they wish that time would stop. When they are at school, time cannot pass quickly enough. Children never seem to complain about wasting time at school when they are doing the things they want to do. And are we any different?

We seem obsessed with time at work. People clock in and clock out. Employment contracts stipulate how much time you are required to work. Some people work over-time, and others save time up in small parcels, taking it in one whole lump some time later. Athletes spend their whole lives trying to knock a second off their best time, and the difference between winning and losing can be a hundredth of a second. The shelves of business bookshops are filled with books on time management. It is just that we do not seem to have enough time to read them.

Whatever it is, one thing is for certain – time passes and is beyond our control. We cannot stop it, buy it, borrow it or create it, and more importantly – you have no idea how much time you have. There is a limited amount of time allotted to us all, and the problem is that you do not know how much.

Some people try to reduce the effects of time by spending large sums of money on things like rejuvenating creams, or living the good life. There is nothing wrong with either, but there is also no guarantee that whatever you do will give you more time. The papers are full of good-looking healthy people dropping dead. I accept that staying up all night, smoking 100 cigarettes a day and drinking a bottle of vodka will not improve your chances of eking out a bit more time, but I have met some individuals upon whom it seems to have little effect!

Think about what you have wanted to do in your personal life – moving house, buying a bigger car, meeting someone or writing a book. What about work – promotion, selling a big contract or getting to see that important decision maker in that company? Now think about what has stopped you from achieving these goals? I will bet it is time. You simply have not had enough time. There has not been enough time available to get around to doing anything about it. When you have got time, you're going to sit down and do something about it. Tomorrow – right? Or maybe even Monday. Mondays are great days to start doing something about a goal. After all, there are so many of them, and if you miss one week – there is always another one next week. With any luck, it might be a holiday, then you can justifiably put off the start again.

The problem with not having started on a goal has nothing to do with the lack of time, but more to do with the failure to set deadlines. If you do not set deadlines, the only way in which you will achieve a goal is by luck, and that is no achievement at all. Without a deadline, there is no urgency. Without a deadline, then there is always tomorrow. It is a strange thing that the greatest period of activity in a football match is reserved for the last 10 minutes when it suddenly begins to dawn on the teams that the end of the game is near.

FIFTEEN MINUTES COULD CHANGE YOUR LIFE

Getting up 15 minutes earlier in the morning. Going to bed 15 minutes later at night. Watching 15 minutes less television per day. Dozing 15 minutes less a day. These four small changes would gain you one extra hour per working day.

Do you know how many hours a day the average person spends watching television, playing video games, using a mobile, or surfing the internet? Four hours. That is 20 hours a working week, excluding the weekend. That is nearly 120 working days a year. That is half a working year. Over 10 years, some people waste five working years doing nothing in particular!

No wonder some people do twice as much as others, and in the process, achieve twice as much. Even if you just make better use of one hour a day, that is five hours a week, 20 hours a month, 240 hours a year, 10 days gained already. Imagine getting a 10-day start over the competition. They would find it hard to catch you up, wouldn't they? What about doubling it? Where could you get another 10 days?

Start work 15 minutes before everybody else, and finish work 15 minutes later. Take 15 minutes less in breaks, and spend 15 minutes less talking to colleagues about the weather, or what was on the television – anyway, as you are not watching so much anymore, there is less to talk about. Even with these simple ideas, that is 20 extra working days per year. Over 10 years, it is the equivalent of living one year longer than anybody else. If you could live one year longer than anybody else, what would you be able to achieve?

During the 15-minute half time break, a football manager can turn a losing team into a winning team. During the same 15-minute break, a winning team can become over-confident, lose sight of the game, and end up losing.

The 15 minutes before a sales call, and the way you spend it, could mean the difference between winning and losing. Losers spend the time driving to the call listening to the radio or music. When they get into the call, the last thing on their mind is the weather, or the price of fuel, or what is number one in the music charts. Winners take that 15 minutes to relax, and read their sales script, or tell themselves over and over again how good they are, and what a great job they are doing. Do you know that, in 15 minutes, you can say "I love this job, and I am a winner" 300 times?

The winners in any field invest just 15 minutes longer than the losers. Fifteen minutes after the others have given up, the winners are still pitching. Practising for 15 minutes each day is over an hour's more practice in a working week than 99.9% of salespeople spend in practice in a year.

At 15 minutes a day, you could practice your skill for a total of 91 hours a year, which would be like practising non-stop for nearly four days and four nights. If you do anything for four days and four nights without stopping, you must be better at it at the end of that time.

Those that take the lead in any field are not geniuses, nor do they come from the top strata in society. Most human endeavour and most of the advances in all walks of life and in all sciences have come from the working classes. Not because they were any brighter, and certainly not because they were born with silver spoons in their mouths. Becoming a lead in any field requires an investment of time and of hard work, but not so much as to make it unattainable for most of us. It is possible to become the best you can possibly be at what you do through investing 15 minutes a day in rehearsing to become better at what you do.

Time is the single most expensive commodity in the universe. It is more precious than all of the gold, diamonds or platinum that have been, and will ever be, in existence, and it is all yours.

USING TIME EFFECTIVELY

Effective use of time has nothing to do with completing time management systems. These are meant to help you control the time you use, or to help you make more effective use of your time. For a tiny minority of you, these systems may work; for the vast majority, the chances are you cannot remember where you put the thing. For a large number of people using these time management systems, time has become a process of filling in boxes, crossing out tasks, and eventually achieving nothing more than passing time. Some people I know seem to spend their whole lives filling in these time management systems to the extent that it is difficult to determine who is managing whom. Systems are not going to help. Time is too short to be filling in pages and pages of information. Life to me is a bit more than having it filled up with appointments to speak to other people.

In some companies, the paranoia with time management systems reaches the ridiculous. In one company in which I worked, I watched a secretary asking someone whether he could make an appointment to see her boss – he had a window in his diary (I love this phrase – a window – yuck!) in three weeks' time. He replied, "If it's not that important, then we don't need to make an appointment. Get him to call me". The matter was resolved on the telephone in a matter of minutes. There are some people whose lives are so full of meaningless appointments that they lose sight of what life is all about.

The vast majority of inter-office emails are created by people with nothing better to do than to waste your time.

Think about the last time you came back from holiday. What happened to most of the mail you opened on your return – it ended up in the trash. You could save yourself the time by putting it there in the first place! Fill your day up with things you want to do – it will make you feel better, and you will achieve 10 times more than those people writing to you. Use your time for yourself.

If you want to get through all the items on your daily to-do list, you should only programme 60% of your time to doing it. Some people recommend 50%. There are always unpredictable events during the day – emergencies, interruptions, fatigue, and loss of concentration. Trying to plan down to the minute is unrealistic, and at best naive. For example, it would be silly to set up four half-hour appointments in a two-hour period without allowing at least a few minutes before each one to look over any relevant documents and to make notes.

WASTING TIME

The sorts of things that waste our time include:

- Not planning ahead, and therefore involving yourself in crisis management.
- Biting off more than you can reasonably cope with, and then spending more time panicking than actually doing; you become like the rabbit in the headlights.
- Spending more time worrying about completing a task than actually doing something constructive about it.
- Moving around from one task to another without actually completing any of them. People will only remember things you have done, not things you are in the process of doing.
- Failing to set priorities, and therefore working on minor items that are not important. When time is short, only work on things that are important, and will move you towards your goal.
- Trying to be a perfectionist.
- Trying to please everyone by always saying "Yes".
- Working on minor tasks because they are easier to do, and the big task would take too long – and you have not got enough time.
- Spending too much time in social chat instead of getting to the point. Are you trying to be popular or successful – the two do not always go together.
- Attending too many useless meetings.
- Failure to organise, and therefore spending more time looking for something than using something you need, to complete a task.

One way of analysing your time is periodically to complete **Table 8** below by inputting how many minutes per day you spend on the activities listed.

Add any other activities you feel are relevant. If most of your time is not spent selling face-to-face with customers, then there is something wrong, and you will never achieve the success you desire.

ITEM	DAY 1	DAY 2	DAY 3	DAY 4	DAY 5	WEEK TOTAL
Face-to-face with customers						
Prospecting – research						
Prospecting – telephoning						
In the car						
Socialising with customers						
Socialising with colleagues						
Waiting to see customers						
Composing and writing emails/letters						
Completing administration						
Meetings						
Training						
Rehearsing						
Thinking time						

Table 8: Your Personal Time Record

DO IT NOW

Whatever it is you need to do, do it now. Do it, and think about it later. If something needs doing, do it. Or at least do something that moves it along. Do not think, just do it. Everything that needs doing, do it. If it is something that can wait, it is probably not worth doing, so forget it – get rid of it. It is amazing how many things in your life – and especially in your work – are useless time wasters. People who use time effectively do not use time management systems; they do not have a secret way or organising time; and they do not work every hour that God sends. They just sort out what is a priority and what is not, and they make sure they do the priorities. They ask themselves regularly, "Is what I'm doing now important to me? If not, is what I am doing now going to help me get what I want? If not, is what I am doing now useful and purposeful?" If the answer to all these questions is "No" – especially the last one – stop what you are doing, and do something else.

There are only 24 hours in every day. The vast majority of our working lives are spent in doing things for other people, like employers. By the time you have finished giving your employers what they want, there is not a lot of time left for you yourself. In fact, some jobs are so demanding that there is no time left for a private life at all. That is why it is important to ask yourself every day, "Is this job giving me what I want?" If you are not achieving the level of success you believe you should be; if you are unhappy about going to work every day; if life is slipping away – and you cannot work out why – it is time you started thinking about the time you are wasting, the time you cannot recapture, the time to change.

You cannot recapture the time that has gone, but you can use the time to come, to change your life for the better. It does not mean writing down and planning each hour of each day, because that rarely works.

Before you go to work, say to yourself, "I will use my time to a greater effect today than I did yesterday. The time I spend today will be quality time. In the roughly 16 waking hours in this day, I will achieve more than most people achieve in 16 days. My time is precious, and I will treat it accordingly, giving it respect and cherishing each moment I spend".

The key thing to remember is that anything is achievable, whether pressurised by the inevitability of time or not, simply by the process of setting deadlines. Deadlines force you to make use of available time, and help you to organise your resources. And people who USE time, act as though they have a limited amount of it left.

One of the best books on time management is by Alan Lakein.[50] Highlights from the book include the following advice:

- List your goals and set your priorities.
- Decide your long term goal.
- Decide what you want to do in the next six months.
- Make a daily To Do list.

---

[50] Lakein, A. (1984). *How to Get Control of Your Time and Your Life*, London: Gower.

- Start with As not with Cs.
- Ask yourself often "What's the best use of my time right now?"
- Do it now.
- You cannot stop time, so do not waste it.
- There are only 24 hours in each day and only 168 in a week. Live each day.

NEXT ...

- How often do you hear someone at work say that they do not have enough time, and then on another occasion say there is plenty of time to do a particular project?
- How often did you have something to do, put it off because you thought you had plenty of time, and then suddenly realised that time had caught up with you, and you had to rush the job?
- What would happen, if half way through a project, you were only given half as much time again to finish it?

PART TWO

ADVANCED SELLING SKILLS, KNOWLEDGE AND AWARENESS

CHAPTER 12
SALES NEGOTIATION SKILLS

SUMMARY

- Negotiation involves creating a WIN-WIN outcome for you and the customer.
- The key to negotiation is preparation. You need to do your homework thoroughly about both your own, and your customer's, potential selling and buying limits of authority.
- Come to a decision regarding the compromises that are to be made, and determine their financial repercussions, both on you and your customer.
- Prepare to make clear your position in the negotiation process.
- Look at the ways in which you are going to execute and subsequently finish the entire negotiation.

Let us never negotiate out of fear, but let us never fear to negotiate. J.F. Kennedy

My dictionary defines negotiation as 'conferring with another with a view to compromise'. However, most salespeople have little or no authority to negotiate, whether on price, delivery or quality.

We usually hear of negotiations taking place where two sides are in disagreement or conflict. Whilst there should not be a conflict between a buyer and a seller, there are times when it can feel as though a struggle is taking place.

Negotiation is a process that uses basic level selling techniques as a foundation, and focuses on the more fundamental needs of the customer, rather than a simple "Yes" or "No" answer. It is the 'clinching factor' that fills the gap between the salesperson and the buyer, during the sales process. The fundamental difference between selling and negotiation is the composition of the eventual outcome for both parties concerned. With selling, the focus remains on the specific advantages associated with products and services. In the process of negotiation, the emphasis is on the impact on profitability, and also the potential lessening in costs to both parties at the end of the discussions.[51]

Negotiation is a process whereby both sides involved draw up a number of proposals and objections until a compromise is achieved. This not only benefits the customer, but also ensures that the salesperson can maximise profitability for his/her organisation.

I define negotiation as 'a process of discussion which moves the opening positions to one where business is transacted, the conditions of which are acceptable to both parties'.[52]

NEGOTIATION MIGHT NOT BE POSSIBLE

There are times when negotiation is either simply not possible or is inappropriate. The customer may put discount demands to you that would be suicidal for your company. Many companies have fallen into the trap of accepting terms from customers either to keep an account or to save turnover.

Selling your products at anything other than a profit makes no business sense whatsoever. Unless, that is, you can guarantee that when a customer buys a product from you at cost, or even at a loss, they will buy other products from which you will make sufficient profit to cover the lack of profit from the other sale. Companies sometimes call this type of activity 'loss-leading'. Unless you know exactly what you are doing, it is a risky practice.

You should not enter into negotiation if:

---

[51]   Lidstone, J. (1991). *Manual of Sales Negotiation*, London: Gower.
[52]   Salisbury, F. (1995). *Negotiating Sales*, Manchester: Development Processes.

- **You do not have enough information to proceed:** In negotiation, information is power. If you do not have any and the customer has, it is almost certain that you will lose. You may make a profit, but chances are it will be nowhere near what you could have made with prior information.

- **You have not prepared in advance:** Whether your preparation is mental or physical, whether your preparation involves attaining the right attitude or getting together the papers you need for the meeting, failure to prepare is tantamount to not negotiating at all. You can be sure that the customer prepares.

- **There is no need to negotiate:** If the customer is prepared to buy at your first price, why bother? Yet there are plenty examples of salespeople whose opening gambit is often "... and if you buy 'x' amount from me I can give you a discount of ...."

- **The customer's demands are totally unacceptable:** If you know that the final position that the customer will adopt with you is unacceptable to your company, then you should say so and withdraw.

- **You do not have the authority:** There is nothing more likely to ruin relationships with customers than when salespeople enter into negotiations and then explain that they have to seek final authority from someone else.

THE PROCESS OF NEGOTIATION

There are obviously two sides to any sales situation (see **Figure 35**). You want to sell at the best price (A), making the most profit, whilst the customer wants to buy the best product at the cheapest price (B). The struggle could involve you getting what you want, and at the same time, allowing the customer to have what they want. The two positions may seem incompatible.

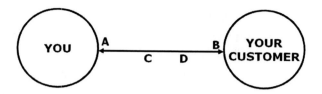

Figure 35: Negotiating Positions in a Typical Sales Situation

If you start at position A and the customer is at position B, what are positions C and D? Most people say that position C represents your compromise and position D the customer's possible compromise.

Now consider: "What if your company had carefully worked out its pricing structure which had to remain at A? Could you get the customer to move to your A position? What if the customer's company policy was to buy goods only at point B?

If your company has a policy of not giving a discount under usual payment terms of 30 days from invoice for payment (which was the bottom price for making a profit), what would you say to a customer who proposed giving you cash on delivery if you gave a discount? Is it the buyer or the seller who has the stronger position? It depends on the uniqueness of the product, and the existence of competition. So, in many ways, it might be argued that, after all, compromising might not be a desired element of the negotiation process, since in order to expedite business, somebody, somewhere, has to give ground.

Perhaps a better definition of negotiation might be:

A process of communication between seller and buyer which moves from an apparent opposing opening stance, to one where the sales terms of the business transaction are acceptable to both parties.

The ultimate success of negotiation is determined by three factors:

- Understanding what the best outcome for you would be, and where the absolute bottom line is.
- Your understanding of the strengths and weaknesses of the customer's buying position.
- Your determination to walk away if the deal is unacceptable.

There are four possible outcomes to any negotiation situation:

- **Win-Win:** You and the customer both get what you want, or at least come away happy with your respective deals, having had the opportunity to both give and receive concessions.

- **Lose-Lose:** You and the customer fail to reach agreement, resulting in you not selling your product, and the customer not buying what they really want. In some cases, this might make both of you worse off.

- **Win-Lose:** You get what you want, but even if the customer ends up buying your product, they feel cheated or exploited. This usually results in one-off sales where the customer keeps searching until they find a new supplier for their next transaction.

- **Lose-Win:** You end up selling at disadvantageous terms. The customer wins, but may lose out in the end if you decide not to engage in the future, or worse still, that this sort of business harms your trading position to the extent that you are not around the next time the customer wants to buy. This position can and does happen, but it is very difficult to get some customers to agree that this is not desirable. Experience shows that good customers are as interested in keeping good suppliers in business as much as attempting to get the cheapest price for the highest quality goods.

THE BEST OUTCOME AND THE ABSOLUTE BOTTOM LINE

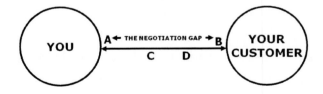

Figure 36: Identifying the Negotiation Gap

If position A in **Figure 36** is determined by your company to be the position at which it makes the optimum profit, then this is called the 'best outcome'. If position B is determined to be the position at which your company makes no profit at all, then this is called the 'worst outcome'. In between these two positions is the 'negotiation gap'.

If position A is a sale at €1,000, from which you make €500 profit, and position B is the same product which the buyer is prepared to purchase at €500, then the negotiation gap equals €500 (€1,000 - €500 = €500). The area between the two points is represented in **Figure 37** by the area PAB.

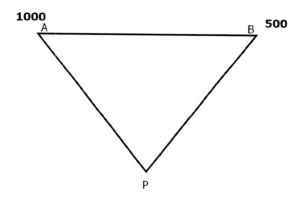

Figure 37: The Negotiation Gap I

What the negotiator must do is to determine where along the A and B axis their absolute bottom line is. To plot this, you need to know two things:

- What is your company's ideal profit margin from the sale?
- What is the least acceptable profit margin?

Ideal profit margin - best outcome

If your company's aim is to add a 60% profit margin on a product that cost €500 to make and distribute, you could discount to €800 (€500 + 60% of €500), which is point E (see **Figure 38**). This then establishes the first point of negotiation – the best outcome – selling at €800.

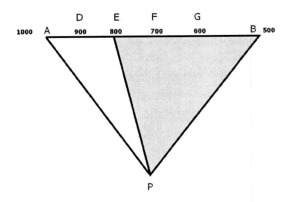

Figure 38: The Negotiation Gap II: The Best Outcome

Least acceptable profit margin - absolute bottom line
Suppose that trading conditions are difficult, and your company would accept an absolute bottom line profit of €100, which would be at point G (**Figure 39**). The parameters of your negotiation stance are therefore PEG and its value is €200 (the difference between G and E).

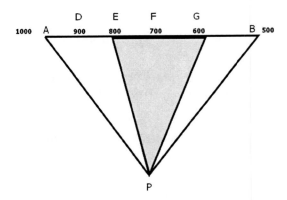

Figure 39: The Negotiation Gap III: The Seller's Absolute Bottom Line

Small movements in price, therefore, can have a dramatic effect on the percentage of margin.

The strengths and weaknesses of the customer's position
The last piece of information needed to establish the actual negotiation area is the buyer's absolute bottom line.

Suppose that the customer in this scenario has another supplier they can buy from at €600, but they know that the quality of your product is superior. They are prepared to put a premium of €100 on that quality. Thus the absolute bottom line for them is a purchase price of €700, which falls into the area PBF (**Figure 40**). In this situation, you both might be open to negotiate over a difference of €200. The problem is that neither of you know what the other is prepared to give or take.

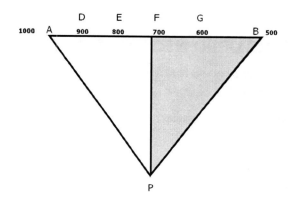

**Figure 40: The Negotiation Gap IV: The Buyer's
Absolute Bottom Line**

To find out the scope of possible negotiation, you might begin by asking the customer: "Are you in a position to make the buying decision, or do you make recommendations to someone else?"

It is worth establishing whether your customer is a decision-maker or an influencer. If they merely influence the sale, then you should not give too much away about the final price or discount you might offer. Negotiations should only take place between decision-makers. It would be pointless for you to enter negotiations with a customer only to be referred to someone else. You would end up having to start all over again, probably from a weaker starting position.

A SWOT analysis

You also need to examine the strengths and weaknesses of your negotiation position, and the strengths and weaknesses of the customer's negotiation position. Additionally, consider what alternatives you think the customer has. Your strengths may include quality, price, locality, distribution, and availability. Each of these is worth something. Correspondingly, the weaknesses of your case could reduce the power you have to negotiate. You should take time to find out about your customer, and what cards they hold. This is where networking with others is so important. You should also read the local and trade press regularly in order to be well informed about your customer.

A STRUCTURED NEGOTIATION PROCESS

A standard six-stage process for negotiation is:

1. Set realistic objectives.
2. Ask questions about the customer's negotiating position.
3. Make an opening offer.
4. Listen, and if necessary, make concessions.
5. Review your position and that of the customer.
6. Make a final offer, and stick to it.

1. Set realistic objectives

In negotiation, planning is everything. Think about what you want to say, how you intend to say it, and practise it until it the process is innate. You should sound and look confident when you enter into negotiation. Also it is important that you have the authority to negotiate, but do not exaggerate your authority or ability to negotiate.

Set yourself high objectives but make sure that they are realistic. For example, if you know that you normally operate on a profit margin of 20%, which may be the norm for your industry, then it is pointless opening your negotiation at a margin of 50%. You run the risk of putting the customer off immediately, and not being allowed to even get off the starting blocks. Starting off too high also means that, at some stage, you will have to reduce your offer significantly, losing you face in front of the customer. For example, if you normally sell a product at €500, but start off offering a price of €1,000, the customer may know that the average price for the product is €500, and offer €350. Where does this leave you? Coming down from €500 to €350 looks better than coming down from €1,000 to €350.

You need to do your homework about the customer and the competition. Just as you may have some negotiating power, your customer may have a number of alternative suppliers available. Put yourself in the competition's shoes. What would you do, say and offer?

Be absolutely clear about the parameters of your negotiating position. Never negotiate below the figure agreed with your company. And do not fall into the trap of saying to customers who refuse to buy at your price, "I'll ask the boss and get back to you". It will do irreparable damage to your reputation as a negotiator. If you find that you are simply not getting anywhere with your terms and conditions of sale, talk it through with your boss. However, you also should invite the boss to come out with you in order to give you feedback about your negotiation style.

It could be a good idea to mystery-shop the competition. If you are providing services to a retailer, it also may be worthwhile mystery shopping the customer.

Lidstone[53] believes that preparation is everything. He advises that it is important to possess sufficient knowledge about your prospect's business, which can be achieved by researching your prospect's market to discover:

- The changes that are taking place within their market that will justify their purchase of your product.

- Whether they have any information resources concerning the market they operate in.

Then after identifying your prospect's competitors and their potential strengths, you should consider:

[53] Lidstone, J. (1991). *Manual of Sales Negotiation*, London: Gower.

- **The economic state of the country:** Can changes in the country's economy affect your client's business in a negative or positive way? How large a portion of their business is done abroad and at home?
- **Government sanctions:** How do these affect your business in terms of pricing, advertising and products?
- **Technological innovations:** Will the introduction of new technology result in fewer sales for your customer's products or services? Identify the ways in which your new technology can benefit them.

2. Ask questions about the customer's negotiating position

Find out as much as you can before making an offer. Questions include:

- "What are you looking for from this product?"
- "When would you be looking for delivery?"
- "How do you normally pay for supplies?"
- "Where have you been buying this product in the past?"
- "What would make you change your current supplier?"
- "What would you expect to pay for this?"

These, and questions like these, are about establishing whether you have any chance of selling the product at the price you want. Unless the product is unique, and the customer is forced to buy from you, in which case, it is up to the buyer to try and negotiate!

3. Make an opening offer

Your opening offer should be the best outcome for you, but not necessarily the worst for the customer. One of the basic rules of negotiating is that there should be no losers. The paradox is that both sides must win, yet feel that they have not conceded something that the other has won. You should not make an opening offer without having received a great deal of information from the customer. Making an offer should be the customer's reward for having supplied information.

4. Listen to the response and, if necessary, make concessions
It is impossible to listen attentively if you are constantly thinking about what to say. By rehearsing what you want to say, and how you intend to say it, you can concentrate on the customer's reaction to your offer. Negotiation is a 'give and take' process in which the conditions of the sale are agreed, understood, and bargained for by both parties. The need to sell is, by and large, balanced by the need to buy.

Some things will be easy to concede, but others may be impossible. Make sure you understand what you can and cannot negotiate. Plan ahead. When making concessions, it is important not to make all of your possible concessions at once. Make them one at a time, when appropriate. For each concession you make, you want a concession from the buyer. The sort of question you might ask could be: "If I am able to meet that condition, would you be willing to ...?"

5. Review your position and that of the customer
Periodically check out understanding by asking questions such as:

- "Just so I don't misunderstand what you're saying – are you saying that ...?"

- "Let me summarise where I think we are so far?"

- "So what you are saying is?"

6. Make a final offer and stick to it
Never say you are making a final offer, and then make another. The most important point about negotiating is to know when to stay, and when to walk away. If you have already decided that, when you reach a certain point in negotiation, you will walk away from the sale, then you must do so. It should be understood, however, that walking away does not mean confrontation. Whilst it is important to be firm about your final position, it should not be done in such a way as to antagonise your customer. There is always another day.

When you have made a final offer and the customer still does not buy, try and end the negotiation on a positive note, such as the potential to conduct business in the future on more favourable terms. You should always attempt to keep the door open, ending on such statements as: "If at some time in the future I was able to meet your buying position, would you buy from me?"

Beware of 'dirty tricks'

There may be times when you meet a customer whose prime motivation is to win. Sometimes they start by creating an environment in which you are meant to feel uncomfortable, such as choosing where you sit. I recall entering the office of the Regional Manager of a chain of newsagents only to find that the seat I had to sit on was a low armchair in the middle of the room. The customer was behind a big towering desk, with his secretary by his side. To the left of me, and to the right of me, sat a number of his colleagues. It felt like Custer's Last Stand. In fact, I actually said, without sitting down, "This feels like Custer's Last Stand". It brought a laugh and allowed me to follow it up by saying, "Look, I have a proposal to make which I know will be of advantage to you and me. But to deliver it in my best way, I need to arrange the seating slightly differently. If you don't mind, I would like to ..." and I began to organise the room to suit myself. If you are confident and you practise well, the customer will always allow you to arrange the environment to suit you.

If the customer begins by complaining about past service, or threatens to take other business away from you if you do not meet what appear to be unfair demands, then you cannot negotiate until you have settled the problem. You should say something along the lines of: "Mr Brown, I am truly sorry if we have let you down in the past. Clearly I would not be here today if I did not believe that I have a product that would greatly benefit you at a price that is both reasonable, and would add value to your company. However, it appears pointless to talk about that if you are unhappy about something in the past. What I would like to do is to put right whatever the problem is, and then make a further appointment to talk about what I came here to do today. Does that sound reasonable to you?"

If it involves a threat, say, "Mr Brown, I am surprised to hear you say that. The purpose of my visit was to share with you a unique proposition that I know will benefit your company, and add value, irrespective of whether we are already supplying you or not. What I would like to do is to focus on my proposal today, and make an appointment to come back sometime soon to discuss the wider picture. Does that sound reasonable?" This gives you the opportunity to discuss the situation with your manager before getting in too deep.

Last, those who are good at negotiating, and indeed at selling, understand that price is not everything. People do not always buy cheap. Quality and service come at a price. There are no companies that sell high quality goods, backed by impeccable service, at a cheap price.

NEXT ...

- What are the strengths and weaknesses of your negotiation situation?
- What are the strengths and weaknesses of your customer's negotiation situation?
- What is the least you are prepared to accept?

CHAPTER **13**

CUSTOMER SERVICE MEANS MORE SALES

SUMMARY

- The sale is not complete until the customer buys again.
- The customer might not always be right, but they are always the customer.
- Word-of-mouth recommendations are worth more than all the advertising you can afford.
- Excellent service quality can be achieved only by careful planning and implementation of operating systems that can be monitored to ensure that they meet set customer service standards.
- A complaint is a customer communicating their dissatisfaction at the service or product that you have provided. It is an important message that tells you where you are going wrong and gives you vital information about your customer's wants, needs and expectations. You cannot buy this information so you need to respect it and use it!

The only foundation of real business is service. Henry Ford

In many companies, the customer service function sits outside the sales channel. In other companies, the customer service function is seen in some way as being inferior to the sales function. My belief is that customer service is integral to sales success. You need to be heavily involved in customer service. Without good customer service, there will be no repeat sales, and repeat sales are the most profitable revenue any company can generate.

The selling process is not complete merely because the customer has stated that he or she will buy your products or services. Throughout the entire selling process, the maintenance of goodwill is important, but even more so after the purchase. Regardless of your customer's previous feeling towards your company, the experience they have after they have bought has a significant impact on future sales. A worthwhile maxim to adopt is 'a customer cannot be regarded as satisfied until we get their next order'.

In 70% of cases where people have been asked the question "What would you say was the main difference between somewhere where you received good service and somewhere you received poor service?", the response has been "The attitude and behaviour of the person delivering the service".

SALES FOLLOW-UP

A major life insurance company I worked for revealed that, in nearly 60% of all life insurance lapses, the policy terminated after the second premium payment. The same company pointed out that, after a policyholder makes four premium payments, lapses are negligible. The significance of these statistics is that customers must remain convinced that their buying decisions were correct or repeat purchases are likely to stop. Through the final step in the selling process – the follow-up – you can influence the satisfaction your customers derive from their purchases.

The Pareto Principle[54] (the '80/20 rule') used in a sales context states that quite often 80% of our sales come from only 20% of customers. Conversely, on analysis, many salespeople say that 80% of their customer activities result in only 20% of sales. Your time is limited, but time spent with customers is often an investment in greater sales and future profits. Even accounts that are semi-active or lacking in potential might become high volume purchasers if service

---

[54]   Named after an Italian economist, Pareto, who first cited this ratio in relation to land ownership.

and follow-up activities can change their attitudes toward you and your company.

Follow-up activities vary substantially by industry and product. At one extreme, it is unlikely that a Boy Scout selling raffle tickets house to house during his annual fundraising will make any follow-up calls during the year. On the other hand, a retail merchant buying household products for re-sale may require regular assistance from their supplier such as inventory maintenance, merchandise displays, and co-operative advertising programmes, all of which can be part of the follow-up. But even the Scout group will need to deliver the prizes and should publish a list of winners.

Thank you letters

You are far more likely to get repeat orders if you develop an amicable relationship with your customers. Any activity that helps to cement this relationship, from a simple 'thank you' to hand-delivering a substantial order, can benefit both you and your customer. A simple goodwill-builder, but one far too frequently overlooked, is sending a 'thank you' letter or card soon after a sales call has been made. The cost of postage and the time expended are minimal compared to the goodwill that letters or cards can create.

After-sales service and assistance

Even if the product is not delivered in person, a telephone call or an in-person visit may enable you to help your customer with the proper use of your products. Customers who do not know how to use a purchase may blame you or the product for their frustrations and problems. Besides instructing your customers on the proper use of your products, you may also be able to point out additional uses for the items. Sometimes, there may be minor repairs or adjustments resulting from faulty installation that you can correct or arrange service for. In some cases, you may create goodwill just by checking with customers to make certain that their orders were fulfilled and delivered as directed on purchase orders.

You might find these suggestions for follow-up activities useful:

- Make a follow-up 'goodwill-building' visit to your customers within a week after delivery of the product to make certain that the order was fulfilled properly.

- Make certain that the product is satisfactory and is being used properly.

- Offer suggestions to the customer on ways to make more effective or additional use of the product.

- Use the follow-up visit as an opportunity to obtain new prospects – ask for referrals.

- Handle any complaints or misunderstandings as soon as possible and with a positive and courteous attitude.

When you make in-person follow up visits, be sure they are not 'waste-of-time calls'. Before making the call, ask yourself, "How is my customer likely to benefit from this call? What do I want to achieve?" Some small talk is acceptable, but remember that the typical customer probably has little interest in merely killing time.

THE IMPORTANCE OF DEVELOPING ENTHUSIASTIC CUSTOMERS

Enthusiastic customers are one of your best sources of prospects because they are excited about what they buy and want to share that excitement with others. Because of our natural reserve that is not something we do lightly, so we always take notice if a colleague or friend speaks highly of a company.

If you deliver what customers want at a fair price, without any problems, they most likely will be satisfied. Although that is better than being dissatisfied, you need more than this to ensure keeping the customer and increasing sales. You have to develop customer enthusiasm about your products and services. You must deliver more than the customer expects. This breeds enthusiasm, which produces a climate that ensures loyalty and increased sales and recommendations to others.

Here are some suggestions for producing and maintaining enthusiastic customers:

- **Keep in touch:** Check after delivery to see that things are going well. Check again later and ask for leads on new prospects. Write a 'thank you' letter or make a telephone call.

- **Handle complaints promptly:** Problems are inevitable. Do not ignore them; they grow with neglect. Do more than the customer expects in satisfying the complaint.

- **Be a friend:** Think of the customer as a friend and do things for them accordingly. Send birthday cards or postcards while you are on holidays. Congratulate him or her on awards or advancement.

- **Give praise when it is due:** Look for things for which you can give legitimate praise – something the firm has done, awards, increased earnings, or a big order. Customers appreciate attention too.

- **Send prospects to your customers:** If your customers are in business, send leads or refer prospects to them. It is human nature to respond in kind to anyone who does us a favour.

THE COMPETITION

Learn as much as you can about the competition's products and services. Study how they bring their products to market, their policies, their pricing levels or strategies, the markets they serve, and their customers. Use this information to carry out a SWOT analysis as described in **Chapter 10**.

Then:

- List the strong selling points of your competitors and, next to each item on the list, a similar or better customer benefit from your own product or service. Do not assume that every prospect or customer of yours knows your competitors' strong points. Emphasise your own customer benefits during the sales call. Do not mention, or sell, your competitors.

- Analyse why prospects or customers are buying from competitors and prepare a detailed plan to convince them that they should be buying from you instead.

- Continually review and reinforce the reasons why your customers are doing business with you.

- Continually strive to build a close relationship with your customers so they can be more dependent on you.

- Earn the right to ask for more orders based on your commitment to service. Remember: your best customers are probably your competitors' best prospects. Keep working to keep them satisfied and buying from you.

A competitor's customers are loyal and satisfied because the products or services they receive fit their organisation and requirements now. These conditions can, and do, change so customer satisfaction is relative.

BECOMING A PREFERRED SUPPLIER

When competing against established suppliers, you first may have to get on the list of acceptable suppliers. To do so this, you must create awareness and then an interest and desire for your products or services.

Consider sending copies of advertisements, newspaper articles, or trade journal reports in which you and/or your company appears, to your prospect. Use testimonial letters and recommendations. This will alert your prospect to your acceptance by other companies in the same or similar activities.

Invite members of the prospect's firm to visit your plant, your headquarters, your offices, customer installations, or trade shows.

Suggest that their present suppliers are quoting a fair price; however, with new products and services continually being introduced, inflation, improved efficiency, higher productivity, maybe you can do better.

Ask for a copy of their bid specifications and requirements so you can prepare a proposal and quotation for their review and evaluation.

Suggest that they can determine whether what you have proposed will give them more value for money. Offer them:

- Trial orders.

- Sample equipment.
- Thirty-day service evaluation period.
- Money back guarantees.

These are all part of what it may take for you to become an acceptable supplier. Your creativity as a sales professional will be really challenged by thinking of ways and means to become an acceptable supplier to prospects that are apparently satisfied by their present suppliers.

HANDLING COMPLAINTS

'We don't have problems, we have opportunities': a cliché, but very true in the case of complaints. It has been estimated that only one in 20 customers complain when they get bad service; the vast majority just go elsewhere! Worse still, the average person tells nine other people about the bad service they received; they tell everyone but you. A complaint therefore is an opportunity to identify ways of improving your services and hence the goodwill of your customers.

A recommended approach to handling complaints is to:

- Assure the customer that you want to put matters right as soon as possible. This alone will take the steam out of most complaints. After all, it is what the customer wants.
- Thank the customer for bringing the matter to your attention.
- Allow the customer time to explain what the problem is.
- Sympathise with how the customer feels.
- Apologise if it is clearly your company's fault.
- Explain what actions you intend to take.
- Carry out those actions as a matter of extreme urgency.
- Keep the customer informed.

When the complaint is received over the telephone:

- Note down the facts.
- Summarise your understanding of the facts back to the customer to ensure clarity.

- Phone the customer back when you said you would.

- If you have not been able to solve the problem by this time, give a progress report.

REGAINING LOST CUSTOMERS

All organisations lose customers, some for very genuine reasons such as relocation or closure. Sometimes though, customers go either because we do something wrong or a competitor makes a better offer.

After losing a customer to a competitor, ask yourself:

- "What can I do to get this customer back?"

- "What has to be done to assure myself I do not lose more customers for similar reasons?"

Prepare a list of all the things that could have gone wrong with the account. Consider the following:

- Have you kept them abreast of all your new products or services?

- Have you kept them abreast of important price, personnel or policy changes?

- Have you visited them on a frequency appropriate for their business activity?

- Have you considered all the ways of helping them improve their businesses by emphasising products and services that would help them in the marketplace?

Next, set up a convenient meeting with your former customer for a frank discussion so you can clarify the position. Consider key areas such as price, delivery, proper handling of warranties or guarantees, and service calls. Say that although you have lost this particular piece of business, it is your intention to win it back in the future. You want to gain their support in helping you to identify what went wrong by discussing the problems.

NEXT ...

- Mystery shop your own company.

- Mystery shop the competition.
- Contact customers after the sale to find out what their impression is of your customer service.

Chapter 14

SELF-AWARENESS AS A MEANS OF IMPROVING YOUR SALES SUCCESS

SUMMARY

- Successful selling consists of three major elements:
  - Self-esteem.
  - Self-motivation.
  - The ability to communicate effectively.
- The study of transactional analysis is a useful tool in building confidence.
- Salespeople wishing to become successful need to avoid 'withdrawal' behaviour and 'game playing'.

SUCCESSFUL PERSONAL SELLING

Successful personal selling consists of three major elements, which are within the control of the individual salesperson, and a critical fourth that requires an external influence[55] (**Figure 41**).

The first three elements are self esteem, self-motivation, and the ability to communicate effectively. However, without a fourth element, feedback, which is delivered through the intervention of a sales coach, your chances of success can depend on luck.

---

[55] Salisbury, F. (2011). *Coaching Champions: How to Build a Winning Sales Team*, Cork: Oak Tree Press.

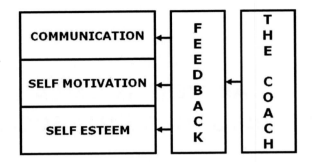

Figure 41: The Elements of Sales Success

Self-esteem

Selling has not enjoyed a particularly positive reputation as a professional occupation. Partly because of this, most people currently in a sales role would not have chosen sales as a career choice. The reality is that many salespeople lack the level of self-esteem that exists in many other professions. This in itself may appear to many to be at odds with the perceived image of the stereotypical often over-confident salesperson.

Self-motivation

Recruitment advertisements for salespeople tend to ask for 'self-motivated' individuals. Yet in most management training programmes, motivating employees is a recurring content theme. That said, many professionals in the fields of sports and the performing arts appear to be driven to succeed – in other words, they are self-motivated.

Communication

Salespeople need to accept that the way in which they communicate with the customer ultimately determines the outcome of the sale.

Effective customer-focussed sales communication involves:

- Establishing common ground with the customer.
- Talking the customer's language.
- Reading and interpreting customer responses.
- Exploring solutions with the customer.

- Building long-term customer relationships.

The coach

The sales coach can, and does, add a critical element to the overall success of individual salespeople. Whilst the preceding three elements of self-esteem, self-motivation, and communication are all prerequisites for sales success, they also can act as barriers (**Figure 42**).

COMMUNICATION	*Lack of Feedback*
SELF MOTIVATION	*Lack of Focus*
SELF ESTEEM	*Self Doubts*

Figure 42: Barriers to Sales Success

A lack of self-esteem can produce feelings of self-doubt. The lack of self-motivation can lead to a lack of focus. A lack of feedback can leave the salesperson unaware of the effect that their behaviour has on the customer. The sales coach, through a series of interventions, helps the salesperson to accept responsibility for their actions, and in doing so, prepares the ground for increased sales performance.

TRANSACTIONAL ANALYSIS

Our attitude determines our behaviour and, therefore, ultimately determines our success or failure. Developing the right attitude is a difficult and perhaps impossible task. People who display a positive attitude are not necessarily feeling positive. In an almost Pavlovian manner, some people learn to display the attitude and behaviour expected of them.

A deeper understanding of attitude and behaviour can be gained by a study of transactional analysis (TA).[56] [57] From a personal perspective, I found the study of transactional analysis to be one of the greatest lessons I have ever learned in the search for better communication skills in selling.

A good way of understanding TA on a very simplistic level is to imagine that everything we have ever experienced, heard, and seen is recorded in the brain. Events that take place during the first seven to nine years of life are said to have a dramatic and lasting effect on us. In later life, the recording of these events is played back from time to time. A current-day event sparks off a reaction that, in turn, plays the tape. Without knowing the reason why, we react to situations in varying ways, either positively or negatively. Using TA techniques, it is possible to gain a clearer understanding of why we feel the way we do in certain situations, what makes us say some of the things we do (and sometimes regret), and what forces us to act in ways that at times border on being personally destructive.

In the process of daily communication, these messages from our past sometimes get in the way of what we are trying to achieve. Depending on our own personal tape of recorded encounters, each of us can react differently when speaking to the same customer. Observers also have personal perceptions which, when combined with the stressful sales situation, can give a totally different view of the sales encounter from that experienced by the salesperson.

In attempting to explain the theory of transactional analysis, Eric Berne devised the concept of 'ego states' – the Adult, the Parent, and the Child. The theory holds that we each have a PAC profile[58] (**Figure 43**), which determines how we think, feel, and behave. The Parent ego state has been learned from our observation and interaction with people who have been our parents, guardians, or figures of authority from our past. The Adult ego state is the way in which we deal with

---

[56]   Berne, E. (1964). *Games People Play: The Basic Handbook of Transactional Analysis*, New York: Ballantine Books.

[57]   Villere, M.F. and Duet, C.P. (1980). *Successful Personal Selling through TA*, Upper Saddle River, NJ: Prentice Hall.

[58]   **Parent Adult Child.**

the here and now. The Child ego state is the replayed feelings, behaviours, and thoughts from our childhood.

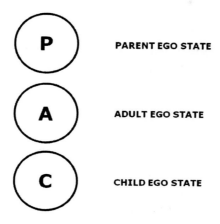

Figure 43: A PAC Profile

Contamination or exclusion

Although we attempt to communicate from the Adult ego state, the influence of our Parents, and of our Childhood reactions to them, in some instances can 'contaminate' the way in which we communicate now. In these instances, we may perceive that we are communicating from a particular ego state and in a particular manner, but because of the contamination we actually communicate with elements of other ego states (**Figure 44**).

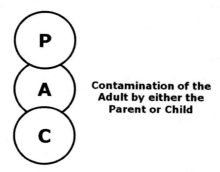

Figure 44: A PAC Profile and Contamination

Not only are there potentially contaminated ego states but some people display a completely inflexible style of communication – one or more of the ego states might be completely missing.

Two sides to the parent

In addition, Berne proposed that there exist two facets to the Parent ego state, namely a 'nurturing parent' and a 'critical parent' (**Figure 45**).

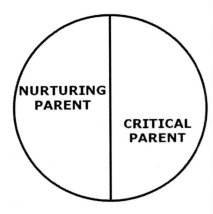

Figure 45: The Parent Ego State: Nurturing and Critical

The Nurturing Parent side of our profile replays feeling and messages of being looked after or cared for, being guided or given advice, of being protected. The Critical Parent side of our profile replays feelings and messages of being told what to do: criticised, admonished, of having limits and rules set upon us, of being judged or disciplined.

Likewise, there are two sides to our Child Ego State: the Free Child and the Adapted Child (**Figure 46**). The Free Child side of our profile recalls feelings and messages of being impulsive, spontaneous, and happy. It recalls feelings of sudden delight and enjoyment, as well as rejection and frustration. The Adapted Child is more complex and recalls ways in which we might have modified our behaviour in order to get what we wanted and avoid what we did not want.

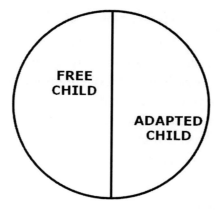

Figure 46: The Child Ego State: Free Child and Adapted Child

Modes

The ego states described have been further subdivided by Susannah Temple,[59] who proposed the word 'mode' as a description of the way in which we communicate, and that there were potential negative or positive 'modes' that we find ourselves in, namely:

- The negative controlling parent is a disciplinarian.
- The negative nurturing parent is over-protective.
- The negative free child runs wild with no thought to others.
- The negative adapted child suffers from anxiety and depression.
- The positive controlling parent offers constructive criticism.
- The positive nurturing parent is caring.
- The positive free child is creative and fun loving.
- The positive adapted child tries to play to the rules.
- The middle road is described as the 'accounting mode', which chooses which mode it is best to operate from in order to communicate effectively.

---

[59] Temple, S. (1999). 'The fluency model', *Transactional Analysis Journal*, Vol. 29, No. 3.

TRANSACTIONS

A transaction is defined as a unit of communication, where one or more of our inbuilt ego states communicate with the perceived ego state of another person. This form of communication is usually, but not exclusively, verbal. Conversations, therefore, are made up of chains of transactions, each of which can be independently analysed.

It is possible to classify transactions into three basic types:

- Complementary transactions.
- Crossed transactions.
- Ulterior transactions.

Complementary transactions

When the response to stimulus comes from the ego state we expect it to, and to which it was directed, the transaction is said to be complementary. Complementary transactions are the basis for smooth and effective communication, and so long as the transaction remains complementary, communication will continue. Examples of complementary transactions are shown in **Figures 47** (adult to adult) and **Figure 48** (parent to child).

In presenting these transactions graphically, the stimulus and response lines of communication for complementary transactions are shown as being parallel.

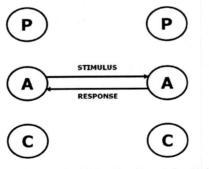

"*Do you know what time it is?*"   "*Yes – it's nearly four o'clock*"

Figure 47: Complementary Transactions I: Adult to Adult

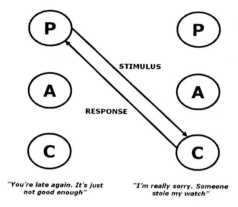

"You're late again. It's just   "I'm really sorry. Someone
not good enough"   stole my watch"

Figure 48: Complementary Transactions II: Parent to Child

Crossed transactions

When the response to a stimulus comes from an ego state other than the expected one, the transaction is said to be crossed (**Figures 49**). At this point, communication is said to be broken or to be in danger of degenerating, and remains so until one or other of the participants alters their ego state.

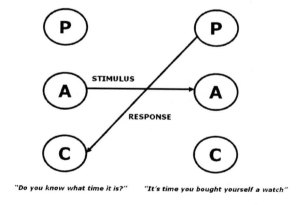

"Do you know what time it is?"   "It's time you bought yourself a watch"

Figure 49: Crossed Transactions

When a transaction becomes crossed, people tend to withdraw; turn away from each other; change the subject; or get upset.

Ulterior transactions

These occur when the spoken words contain a hidden message – when a person says one thing but means something else. The continuous lines in **Figure 50** show the actual conversation. The stimulus is delivered in an even voice. In this instance, the response is not parallel but neither is it crossed. In fact, the response (the dotted line) has come from the ulterior stimulus transaction. In this example, perhaps it is a salesperson, believing the customer to be operating predominantly from the child ego state, implies that the customer cannot afford the item.

Whilst the outcome of the conversation may be satisfactory to the sender, the responder eventually becomes dissatisfied with the outcome and, given enough opportunity to consider why, will trace that dissatisfaction back to the original transaction and the person. People who fall into this trap once, often fall into the same trap time after time. Recognising how this happens and why this happens is the first step in taking control.

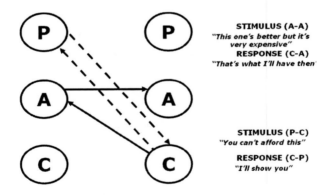

STIMULUS (A-A)
"This one's better but it's very expensive"
RESPONSE (C-A)
"That's what I'll have then"

STIMULUS (P-C)
"You can't afford this"
RESPONSE (C-P)
"I'll show you"

Figure 50: Ulterior Transactions

Ulterior transactions usually involve more than two ego states operating simultaneously. Ulterior transactions form the basis for something known in transactional terms as 'game playing'.

Not what you say, BUT how you say it

It is worth bearing in mind that gestures, expressions, body posture and tone of voice all contribute to the meaning, intended or otherwise, of a transaction. Yet even these can be confusing, if messages from the past have instructed us to behave in particular way – for example, 'don't stare at people; don't talk to strangers; if you have nothing to say – it's better to say nothing'.

FROM TA TO THE SEA SCALE

In many books and articles on TA, it is suggested that you ignore the normal meaning of the words Parent, Adult, and Child, and merely look at these behaviours without saying 'this is the Parent speaking, or this is Child-like behaviour, or this is an Adult behaviour'. Therefore, I have updated the theory of TA to help salespeople understand how both salespeople and customers react in certain sales situations. I found that the existing TA terminology sometimes gets in the way of full understanding. For this reason, I have substituted the Parent/Adult/Child ego states for a Subordinate/Authoritarian/ Egalitarian (SEA) scale, in which the Child ego state becomes the Subordinate role (S), the Parent ego state becomes the Authoritarian or Authoritative role (A), and the Adult ego state becomes the Equal or Egalitarian Role (E) (**Figure 51**).

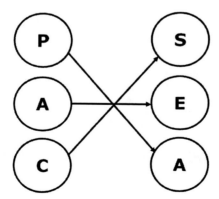

Figure 51: The PAC Profile and the SEA Scale

As salespeople, there are some customers who can make us feel as though we are in a subordinate role to them. It makes us behave in a non-assertive manner. In a similar vein, customers can feel intimidated by an aggressive salesperson. At other times, we may act as though we are authoritative about the product but the customer may misinterpret our desire to appear knowledgeable with a 'smart-Alec' labelling. Likewise, some customers may remind us of the authority figures of our past.

The subordinate salesperson seeks to give the customer whatever they want so long as they buy or promise to buy. The authoritarian salesperson comes across as believing they know what is best for the customer. Ideally, we should be trying to promote a partnership approach, where our standing is equal with the customer. We therefore should act assertively.

Positive and negative roles

I also have adapted part of Susannah Temple's Fluency Modes[60] to define positive and negative elements of the SEA Scale (**Figure 52**).

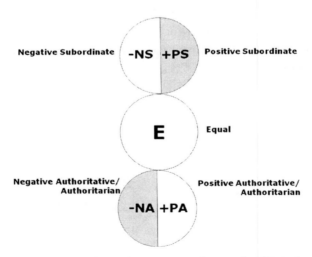

Figure 52: Adapting Fluency Modes to the SEA Scale

---

[60]   Temple, S. (1999). 'Functional fluency modes for educational transactional analysts', *Transactional Analysis Journal*, Vol. 29, pp. 164-174.

This means:

- The negative subordinate role (-NS) displays a significant element of non-assertive behaviour – akin to the Uriah Heep character in *David Copperfield*. The –NS uses self-destructive behaviour to get attention from others – always being late, using delaying tactics, over-compliance or rebellion is typical negative subordinate behaviour.

- The positive subordinate role (+PS) displays the characteristics of someone who is keen to help, and whilst they generally operate in subordinate roles, they do not subjugate themselves by displaying the negative behaviours of their opposite number –NS. The +PS is polite, says the right thing at the right time, expresses their feelings, has fun and does not hurt other people.

- The negative authoritative/authoritarian role (-NA) displays behaviours that leave little doubt as to their personal view of their self-importance. The –NA takes away the self-worth of other people. They also can do too much for other people, leaving them unable to do things for themselves.

- The positive authoritative/authoritarian (+PA) maintains a balance between displaying a leadership function and being aware of the others feelings. The +PA cares for other people when they need it or want it.

Mixed messages

By being more aware of the way in which we communicate and the way in which customers make us feel, we can begin the process of avoiding some of the hurdles and mixed messages that dog our sales interactions, namely:

- **We use the same words but attach different meanings:** We reach agreement but have a differing understanding of the agreement. This is the most common and dangerous form of sales and customer contract confusion, and often leads to a lack of repeat business or no business at all.

- **We use different words but they mean the same thing:** This often leads to a lot of wasted time and unnecessary argument.

STRUCTURING TIME

In Transactional Analysis, there is something called 'Structuring Time', which refers to chains of transactions. Structuring time implies that we are responsible for the manner in which we communicate. In some cases, people structure time in order to interact with other people, and in other circumstances, some people seek to avoid contact. In some situations, people rely on stereotypical pre-set conversations and time-honoured practices in their exchanges with each other. We all tend to respond differently to different situations.

People structure time into six distinct categories:

- Withdrawal.
- Rituals.
- Activities.
- Pastimes.
- Intimacy.
- Games.

Withdrawal

If you have ever attended a meeting with a number of colleagues, you might have noticed people in the state of withdrawal. They are present physically but appear mentally absent. The lights are on but nobody is at home. People in withdrawal find themselves unable or unwilling to participate in communication. They pretend to listen. On the SEA scale, this is defined as NS (negative subordinate) – hidden thoughts can be displayed as forced smiles, wandering attention span, or requiring messages to be constantly repeated. The purpose of withdrawal is to avoid conflict, contact, or doing something that you do not want to do. Some people deliberately engage in withdrawal in order to avoid contact with others. This is especially so for those who regularly have relationship problems with others.

Rituals

Rituals include the way we communicate based upon habit and acting in a way in which we believe we are expected to. Therefore, rituals exist in greetings and farewells, meeting someone for the first time, attending interviews, and the opening of speeches at such events as weddings, birthdays and retirement occasions. What we say and how we say it during rituals depend on how we have been taught to interact with others on a formal basis. Some people are good at this and quickly move onto more personal conversations. Others find rituals uncomfortable or are not good at 'small-talk' and consequently find developing relationships with strangers difficult.

Activities

Activities are closely linked to rituals in that the behaviour we exhibit is learned and, in some cases, might even become habitual. Activities are most often conducted at work as they often involve attempting the achievement of some organisational aim or other. That said activities can also include the achievement of domestic objectives.

Activities include such behaviour as:

- Repeating the same information to others over and over again.
- Using a template to solve relationship problems.
- Appearing busy – but not necessarily being effective.
- Looking after children.

When activities that we have been engaged in for some time come to an end, especially suddenly, it can leave us feeling confused, vulnerable or even depressed.

Pastimes

Pastimes include the sort of conversations that we have with others, which extend beyond rituals to the sharing of some personal likes and dislikes. They include such behaviours as:

- Talking about the weather/sport/what is in the news.
- Sharing prejudices or opinions.
- Holiday stories.
- Office gossip.

Many social events are totally composed of pastimes.

Intimacy

Intimacy or closeness involves transactions of genuine emotion, usually between small groups of people, or couples, where there are no ulterior motives and no hidden agendas. Communication is open and honest. Intimate communication does not necessarily need to involve words but can be evident through looks or touch.

Intimacy includes such behaviour as:

- Sharing problems.
- Two people watching a play or film that both enjoy.
- Comforting others.
- Meeting the gaze of someone else and sharing a moment of enjoyment or even grief.

Some people find intimacy difficult or are suspicious of it. Intimacy can involve personal feelings. Some people feel at ease sharing their innermost thoughts and others are wary of doing so and are suspicious of those who do.

Games

Berne says that some people play psychological games – often subconsciously – and tend to choose as spouse, friends, and even business associates people who will play the role opposite their own. Although there are many different games, in each one there are three basic elements:

- A series of complementary transactions, which on the surface seem plausible.
- An ulterior transaction, which represents the hidden agenda.
- A negative payoff, which concludes the game and is the real purpose for playing.

Games tend to be repetitious. People find themselves saying the same words in the same way, only the time and place may change. Perhaps the replay contributes to what is often described as "I feel as if I've done this before". Games are like short scenes in a life drama.

STROKES AND COLLECTING STAMPS

Strokes

A 'stroke' is any form of recognition given to one person by another. Strokes may be verbal or non-verbal, positive or negative, conditional or unconditional. Everyone needs strokes. It is a human trait to want recognition. The problem is that, if we are not comfortable with positive recognition, we may only accept negative recognition – negative strokes.

There are four basic types of stroke:

- **Positive unconditional:** "I like you".
- **Positive conditional:** "I like you because you do this for me".
- **Negative unconditional:** "I don't like you".
- **Negative conditional:** "I won't like you unless you do this for me".

Different people need different strokes and at varying intensities. Intensity of strokes vary from a 'Good morning' given to a passing acquaintance on the way to work, to 'I love you' to a child, parent or spouse. Positive strokes are authentic, honest, not overdone. They nourish and develop a person. The other person is left feeling good, and important. The feelings behind positive strokes are concerned with good will and the life position of 'I'm OK you're OK'. A life position means the view that we take of ourselves in relation to other people. This probably begins to happen from about the age of 3 to 7 years old. From here on, we are likely to construct a view of world around us to match that life position.

There are four possible life positions:

- I'm OK, you're OK.
- I'm OK, you're not OK.
- I'm not OK, you're OK.
- I'm not OK, you're not OK.

I'm OK, you're OK
This is the ideal, where both people respect each other and their opinions. They accept when they are in the wrong and do not try and embarrass the other person when they appear to be in the wrong. People operating from this position are confident in themselves and their ability to have open communication with others without seeking for hidden meanings.

I'm OK, you're not OK
This is the position of people who put down, victimise, or persecute others. They blame others, often expressing anger, hostility, and impatience. These sorts of people live their lives refusing to look inwardly and to be objective about their own role and responsibilities – problems are always the fault of someone else.

I'm not OK, you're OK
This is a position where people feel powerless or at the mercy of others. Comparisons with others results in inferiority feelings, which can lead to withdrawal, mild depression and an over-dependence on Adapted Child behaviour in formal working settings and Rebellious Child behaviour at other times.

I'm not OK, you're not OK
This is the position of those who lose interest in themselves and in others. In the extreme, individuals may become depressed.

Collecting and redeeming stamps
Collecting feelings from strokes is known as 'collecting stamps'. Stamps from good feelings are 'gold stamps' and from bad feelings are 'black stamps'.

The important point about collecting black stamps is that it is an indulgence in bad feelings learned in childhood which are saved up and redeemed at some point in the future. People tend to collect a favourite bad feeling – not because it is good but because it is familiar. This feeling is usually the same one that they had when things went wrong when they were children. These bad feelings are often collected at the end of a game.[61] People eventually cash in their bad feelings, but the stage at which the collection is redeemed varies from person to person. Some people collect a low number and turn them in for small prizes – a headache, dropping a cup or putting down a shop assistant or bank clerk. The clues to someone cashing in stamps may be some phrases that are often used, "That's the last straw. I've taken all I'm going to. I've had enough".

FOCUS ON THE POSITIVE SIDE OF THE SEA SCALE

The subordinate – S

Many salespeople find the subordinate role difficult to cope with. Any experience of being in a negative subordinate role, where you are there to serve customers, can make you feel in some way inferior. Yet if you talk to people in such jobs as being a butler, they will tell you that it is a profession and that they feel pride in what they do. Martin Luther King said, "If a man is called to be a street sweeper, he should sweep streets even as Michelangelo painted, or as Beethoven composed music or Shakespeare wrote poetry. He should sweep streets so well that all the hosts of heaven and earth will pause to say, 'Here lived a great street sweeper who did his job well'".

The important thing is to feel proud of doing a job well, despite past comments about selling as a career. For many salespeople, these include past messages from parents or guardians encouraging them to seek a career in law or medicine or finance. None of us in selling will have had 'selling' as a career choice presented in the aspirations that our parents and teachers had mapped out for us and it is therefore normal when we become adults to revisit the doubts about selling as an honourable career choice. Some parents also have contributed to building on the negative subordinate role by suggesting that they sacrificed their own career ambitions to give their children a good start in life with opportunities that the parent themselves did not have, "I worked my fingers to the bone to provide

---

[61] See earlier explanation of 'games'.

you with the opportunities I did not have". And then the guilt factor is laid on with "And what thanks do I get from that?"

Allowing these negative messages to run in our heads has the effect of moving you into the 'I'm not OK' quadrants of the life positions mentioned earlier. It can be displayed by behaviour that leads others to believe that either you do not want to be doing the job you have; that you are doing the job under sufferance whilst waiting for something else to come along; or that you find the whole experience of talking to customers pointless.

Positive subordinates have a strong belief in their products and the company they work for. The successful positive subordinate salesperson believes implicitly in what is being sold and this belief rubs off onto the customer. This salesperson employs a balance between logic and emotion. They adopt the attitude that there is no reason why the customer should not see them and their product in a positive light.

The +PS salesperson believes that they are there to serve – not just to sell – however, they also understand that their job is to sell. The – NS salesperson waits for the customer to buy, rationalising to themselves that if the customer does not ask to buy then they do not like the product. The ulterior transaction is "They do not like me".

Most customers expect to be asked to buy. So the +PS seeks to establish from the customer what would make them buy – "Tell me, what would make you change your current supplier and buy from me?"

The –NS salesperson wants to be liked and passionately believes in building rapport, to the extent that most of the transactions are about establishing areas of common interest and providing each other with positive strokes. This can take up so much time that the sales part of the discussion ends up being hurried and lacklustre.

The authoritative/authoritarian – A

This person operates in the 'I'm OK, you're OK' quadrant. They may believe themselves either to be more intelligent or to know more about the product than the customer but their attitude is that they are there to teach the customer about the benefits of their product. They display a genuine concern that they wish to improve the customer's situation. They believe that the customer will be worse off by not buying their product.

The +PA salesperson asks questions that seek to establish what problems the customer may have and works to solve those problems. They provide the customer with positive strokes in order to make the customer feel good about themselves. The +PA salesperson shows an interest in the customer as a person.

The –NA salesperson avoids personal issues and sees non-business conversation as a waste of time, believing that the customer would much prefer to get straight down to business. The +PA salesperson creates a balance between personal and business issues that lean heavily in favour of business solutions but does not ignore the need to display concern about the customer as an individual – not just a buying machine to overcome.

The –NA believes they know what is best for the customer. They see the mistakes the customer is making and they tell them so. They criticise the competition, not realising that this is a slight on the customer's previous buying decisions.

Equal – E

The most professional salesperson sees themselves and the customer as playing equal roles. The customer is trying to do the best for his/her company. The salesperson understands that they have a responsibility to both their own company and the customer. This salesperson understands the value of long-term relationships and that far more profit is made from repeat business than the initial sale.

The E salesperson puts a significant amount of preparation into each customer meeting. They leave nothing to chance. They research the customer and the customer's company prior to any meeting. They put themselves in the customer's shoes and ask themselves such questions as:

- "What would make this customer buy from me?"
- "What benefit could I bring to the customer?"
- "Why is the customer buying from the competition and what can I do about it?"

The E salesperson sees their products from the customer's perspective – warts and all. They sell customers what they want, not what the salesperson believes they should have. The E salesperson does not solely rely on enthusiasm about their product but backs up any benefit statements with factual evidence.

DEVELOPING A WINNING LIFE SCRIPT

Childhood experiences often lock people into scripts. Just as you may play the same game over and over, so you may cast yourself into the same destructive role time and again. You have learned your script from those who influenced you when you were very young. A life script sets out in detail how the course of your life will run. In this way, you may find yourself following the same plan as your parents. Life scripts dictate where you are going and how you are going to get there. They may or may not be the same at home as at work.

The only problems with some of these life scripts is that, having been put together when we were young (anywhere between 7 and 9 years old), they are based on the past. It may turn out that society has changed significantly whereas the execution of our life script is based on attitudes we may have held 10, 20 or even 30 years ago. In addition, the information that we received at this young age has been edited or even censored. We plan out the journey of our lives with only a part of the map. The early script we assembled was done without the benefit of choice.

People of a specific race, background, age, or gender may be scripted by their cultural background to a particular script. Life scripts, therefore, have a tendency to produce behaviours that match the plan of the script. In so doing, it almost becomes a self-fulfilling prophecy. For example, a child may have been exposed to parents who did not get on. Separate messages from each may tell the child a common thread of "Don't trust other people or show them emotion because they will only hurt you". The child may see the parents keeping their distance from each other in order to survive and therefore learns to behave in the same way in order to relate to one or both of them. This childhood decision may be carried into adulthood where it is inappropriate. In this example, a script of 'loneliness' has been established and will be supported by career choices, stamp collecting and negative strokes.

The important thing about scripts, however, is that once you are aware of the source of your script, you can change it. A losing script can be made into a winning script, one where you seek to fulfil your potential. A winning script for a salesperson perhaps should confirm that this is the career you would have chosen had you known more about it when you were younger. The fact that no-one spoke to you about a career in sales means that you understandably did not consider getting into sales until much later. A losing script can result in feelings of "If only ...", "I wish I had ...", or "Yes but ...".

Where are you now and where do you want to be?
One place to start rewriting your life script, based on your chosen career of selling, is to examine which behaviours you find yourself displaying most of the time. In **Figure 53**, I have taken the SEA scale illustration from earlier and converted it into a table.

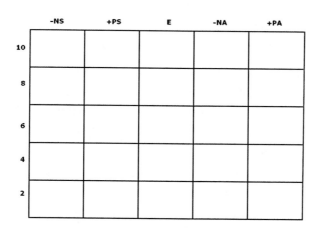

Figure 53: Using the SEA Scale to Create a Personal Development Plan

Using the scale: 0 to 1 = rarely, 2 to 3 = occasionally, 4 to 6 = regularly, 7 to 8 = frequently, and 9 to 10 = consistently, put crosses in the squares corresponding to where on the scale you believe you are.

Then put ticks in the table where you believe you should be in terms of these behaviours. The difference between the two should form your personal development plan for improving your life script.

IMPLICATIONS FOR SALESPEOPLE

By this stage, you may be thinking "This is all very interesting but what has it got to do with improving my selling skills?" Earlier, I proposed that success in personal selling is primarily about the way in which you feel about yourself. Therefore, understanding how those feelings have been developed must be the first step in improving your confidence and self-esteem and hence your sales.

The importance of avoiding withdrawal behaviour
You should keep a record of how much time you spend communicating with other people face-to-face and how much time you spend either in isolation or engaging in activities that are not communicating face-to-face with others such as:

- Sending emails to customers but never following them up with a phone call or visit.
- Writing to customers but not following up.
- Avoiding meetings with colleagues of the boss.
- Inordinate amounts of time reading marketing literature, collecting and collating lists of prospects, writing reports/letters/marketing material/updating charts and sales information, etc.
- Quickly giving up during a telephone prospecting session with excuses like "It's a bad day today, tomorrow will be better".
- Turning back when there is a traffic jam on the way to a customer call.

This type of behaviour primarily emanates from the 'I'm not OK' life position. Knowing that they are 'Not OK', salespeople in this category seek to protect themselves from the disappointment of not making the sale by not putting themselves in the position of being rejected. Inside, there is probably a conversation going on, which says, "If I don't ask the customer for an appointment or a sale – then I can't be rejected".

These salespeople surround themselves with any form of activity that leads them to believe that they are very busy but simply do not have enough time to see customers. Often, they blame the boss and/or the company for creating too much paperwork – for example, "They need to make their mind up what they want me to do – to sell or fill these useless forms in". However, if someone were to call their bluff and remove the necessity to complete that 'useless' paperwork, they would rapidly find some other excuse for not meeting customers.

NEXT ...

- Consider how your 'life script' may affect your communication exchanges with your customers – for better or for worse.

- What are your plans for the next six months to further improve your self-awareness?

CHAPTER 15
MOVING FROM SALES TO SALES MANAGEMENT

SUMMARY

- It is usual for the top salesperson to be promoted to be a sales manager.
- There is no guarantee that top salespeople make good sales managers.
- Sales managers need to have sales experience in order to empathise with the sales team.
- Many of the trait factors that exist in top performers can be barriers to effective sales management.

Individual salespeople tend to aspire to become sales managers. Often this is fostered by companies that provide career guidance specifically focussed on promoting their top salespeople to sales management positions. In many companies, this is seen as an insurance policy, believing that if they do not promote the top salesperson he/she will leave, which causes the second dilemma – by promoting the top salesperson, they will then lose his/her personal sales effort. In this situation, many companies make the biggest mistake of all by giving the newly-promoted sales manager a personal sales target. One issue I need to clear up before going any further: Sales managers should not have a personal sales target.

If you aspire to being a sales manager, then you need to understand that being a player-coach rarely if ever works – as Professor of Marketing at University of North Texas, J.K. Sager, said:

"The best coaches were seldom star players". You either have to be a player or a coach – you cannot do both jobs successfully. As a sales manager, you also have a personal responsibility to help the individuals in your sales team succeed – it is no longer your role to succeed at selling. Your job is to succeed at sales management and sales coaching, and whilst you are playing on the same pitch, you cannot judge whether the team is playing well or not.

What makes you successful at selling will not necessarily make you successful at sales management. Although I believe that sales managers should come from the ranks of salespeople, I also say that being a good salesperson is no guarantee that you will be a good sales manager. Often the more successful you have been at selling, the more difficult it will be for you to manage other salespeople. In some way, the experience of success at selling almost makes us forget what it was like to be unsuccessful – it is almost as though our memories of painful experiences of sales failure are erased, the more successful we become.

Previously, I would have said that the trait of 'personal responsibility' was essential for sales success. Most people who succeed in any walk of life have a sense of personal responsibility for the outcome of their efforts. Salespeople are no different. It is widely assumed that the experience of being successful at sales will ensure the same success in sales management, on the basis that sales success is a transferable trait into sales management (**Figure 54**).

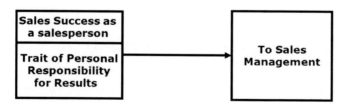

Figure 54: The Transition from Sales to Sales Manager

Yet the 'real' transferable trait is not 'sales success' – which is an outcome – but 'personal responsibility' – which is an input. In this way, the successful salesperson within retains the feeling of personal responsibility for results. Merely operating as a sales manager fails to tap the latent talent and ability of salespeople, unlike sales coaching – which releases the talent within by ensuring that each salesperson in a sales team understands that sales success is exclusively their responsibility. Sales managers are accountable for the performance of the team but not responsible for that performance. The individual members of that team are responsible for their own success and, just as importantly, their own failures. If and when you move into sales management, if you believe and act as though you are responsible for the success or failure of others, then they will allow you to be responsible and that, in itself, will ensure failure in the long term.

WHAT DOES IT TAKE TO BE A GOOD SALES MANAGER?

When I researched the whole subject of sales management a number of years ago, I came across a list compiled by Kimes.[62] He said that managers generally had to have the following 20 attributes:

- Adequate technical knowledge of the area being managed.
- Adept at motivating people.
- Sufficient formal education in order to deal with peers and colleagues successfully.
- An innate managerial mentality, which includes the virtues of being alert, dependable, and willing to carry out a commitment.
- Be a team player, not a grandstander or excessively egotistical.
- The ability to anticipate problems.
- A natural sense of fairness and integrity and be emotionally well-balanced.
- Be courageous, resolute, and willing to demonstrate strength of conviction and a high level of social consciousness.
- Be a good follower and not resentful of instructions or constructive critics.

---

[62] Kimes, J.D. (1988). 'Twenty attributes of an effective manager', *Management Accounting*, July.

- Initiative and be creative, imaginative and resourceful.
- Be energetic.
- A reliable even temperament.
- A competitive spirit.
- A positive attitude.
- Above average communicative skills, be able to write clearly and crisply, speak articulately, and listen intently.
- Not have a deep aversion to administrative duties.
- Understand numbers and know how to use them.
- Be logical and must be capable of making decisions, usually without sufficient information.
- An appreciation for computers.
- Be organised and self-disciplined.

The only thing missing from this list appears to be the ability to leap buildings in one bound! That said, Kimes is not alone developing a list containing such a variety and volume of attributes and personality traits that it leaves you wondering just where these people exist, for it is certain that in 40 years of sales experience I never met any when I was a front-line salesperson or since.

As people move from selling into sales management, they also are exposed to a great number of theories and purported effective practices of sales management. Each is accompanied by a recipe for managerial success, and each one relies on the latest 'new idea'. Enormous sums are spent yearly on management training and development, but recent surveys show that less than one-third of top and middle managers feel that they learned anything important, whether programmes were conducted within their own company, or through outside courses and consultants. The figure for in-house training effectiveness looks particularly bleak at fewer than 10% of managers rating it as effective.

As with sales success, there remains a constant search by trainers, managers, and the jobholders themselves, for the secret of sales management success, although apparently there is the money to pay for it.

Leavitt *et al.*[63] proposes that Zaleznik[64] may be close to the truth when he said that:

> Good management rests on a reconciliation of centralisation and decentralisation, or decentralisation and co-ordinated control: There is no hard and fast rule for sorting out the various responsibilities and the best way to assign them. The balance which is struck varies according to what is being decided, the circumstances of the time, past experience, and the temperaments and skills of the executive involved.

In other words, in the same way that inventors try, fail, try, fail, and continue this process until a solution is found, then good management also must be a process of trial and error. This will not sit well with current day theories of management and yet within this proposal in part lies the answer.

As we already know, the vast majority of people in selling did not want to be salespeople when they were at school, college or university. Most came into it as the doors to other careers closed, either through a lack of qualification or luck. For this reason, a large percentage opts to take sales management roles when the opportunity presents itself in order to satisfy the need for a professional status.

There are three basic skills that sales managers must possess to be successful:

- They must be able to sell.
- They must be able to train and coach.
- They must be able to motivate.

SALES MANAGERS MUST BE ABLE TO SELL

If you want to be successful in sales management, you must know how to sell. You have to be able to get yourself in front of people and

[63]   Leavitt, H.J., Pondy, L.R. and Boje, D.M. (1989). *Readings in Managerial Psychology*, 4th edition, Chicago: University of Chicago.
[64]   Zaleznik, A. (1977). 'Managers and leaders: Are they different?', *Harvard Business Review*, Vol. 55, May/June.

then make a sales presentation that will make people buy from you. Training, coaching and motivation revolve around the basic principle that the sales manager knows how to do it, because at some stage the sales manager might have to demonstrate his or her sales ability and knowledge to the team. So you have to be able to do it. By that I mean that you must at some stage, for at least one week in your sales career, have made the sales target.

Then you will know what success is. That is what success in selling is. It is not about being number one. It is about achieving your target. That is important. You have reached the minimum standard, and that is not easy. You have to understand how good it feels to have done just that, to sell something to someone, and to reach your sales target. Then you can empathise with the salesperson. Empathy is important in selling and it is important in sales management.

Sales managers also have to sell the job. What most sales managers seem to forget is that people need to be sold the job. They expect personnel departments to provide them with salespeople. They expect selection processes to find them ideal candidates. There is no personality trait apart from personal responsibility, and this cannot be measured, it can only be learned. There is no piece of demographic information to help you choose people who will make successful salespeople. It is a sales manager's job to identify people who, in their estimation, will be able to do the job of selling given the right training. That is all it is: an estimation. It is the sales manager who is going to have to work with the salesperson after all.

Selling must be perceived by the candidate to be a professional career. The sales manager must be seen as thoroughly enjoying the job of selling and must give a positive impression.

Interviewing prospective salespeople is an integral and continuous element of the sales manager's job. The turnover of salespeople can be anywhere from 10% to 60% per year – mainly because the majority do not want to be in sales. In some companies I know, it is as high as 80% a year. If a large percentage of the people fail every year, then you are constantly looking for replacements. Never ever assume that your salespeople will stay with you forever. It is not only the failures who leave, it is also the successful people, who are constantly looking around for a better package or a way to get out of sales. Remember that nobody ever got into sales because they wanted to, so the first opportunity that they have to get out, they will take it.

SALES MANAGERS MUST BE ABLE TO TRAIN

What works in sales training? Success in sales training depends on the trainer – not the package, not the content. It is the actual person who does the training that makes the difference. It is the trainer who determines the success or failure of a sales training programme.

The sales trainer has to know what they are talking about. They have to have experience of the subject and to have experienced it first-hand. If you have not been in selling, you are not going to be a good sales trainer. If you have not been in sales management, you are going to struggle relating to trainee sales managers. Without experience, you can only theorise.

You cannot sympathise and empathise with sales managers if you have not been a sales manager yourself. You cannot sympathise or empathise with salespeople if you have not sold. The most effective sales trainer is not a staff trainer or a central or external resource, but the line manager responsible for the salesperson. Ideally, the only person qualified to train salespeople is the sales manager. They have the authority and they are the ones who are ultimately responsible for the development and success of their salespeople.

If your salespeople attend a training course run by someone else, then you should take part in the course yourself – at least once. You must follow it up in the field. So sales managers have to be sales trainers. That gives them credibility. Staff sales trainers do not have the same credibility, because salespeople say that if the sales trainer was any good, then they would be out in the field selling, "If it is such a good job, then why aren't they doing it?"

At some stage, the sales process also has to be demonstrated, which means field training. This is what frightens most sales managers: the fact that, at a certain point on some field visits, a new salesperson will say, "Look, I can't get this right, show me how to do it". At some stage, you might have to demonstrate to your people how it is done, "I'm going to show you how to do it. I'm going to show you how to get that telephone appointment. I'm going to show you how to get commitment from a customer". Salespeople see through sales managers who cannot do the sales job. They have no respect for them at all. They would rather work for sales managers who know how to do the job in practice not just in theory.

Sales managers ought to do field training because they are the ones who understand the problems. How can you understand the problems if you have not done the job? Undoubtedly, salespeople in the field have many problems and most of these are personal and usually stress-related. Sales managers understand the stress and understand that people in the personal selling market have personal problems that are difficult to cope with and which affect the way in which they do the job. Sales managers can discuss these problems with their people in either formal training situations in the classroom, or on an individual basis in the field.

Issues arise on training courses that line managers might never hear. You are dealing with people's personalities and emotions and attitudes. They tend to share confidences with the trainer, so it is better if the trainer happens to be the boss as well, or at the very least the boss is there to observe the interactions.

Insofar as technical knowledge is concerned, then my opinion is that this is best tackled through self-study. The manager sets the salesperson self-study tasks and tests them periodically. At college or university, you do not receive much training. You have to study. You attend lectures. The bulk of learning takes place by self-study. People will only take it on board if they want to.

Surveys into sales[65] and management training[66] clearly show a disappointing reality about the lack of effectiveness of sales training.[67]

[65] Corsini, S. (2005). 'The great sales training robbery', *Training Today*, 1 February.

[66] Anon. (1989). *The Sales Direction Survey of Sales Management*, Sales Direction Magazine/Management Exchange Ltd.

[67] Seabright, P. (2008). *Why Sales Training Doesn't Work*, West Tisbury, MA: ES Research Group Inc.

The fact remains that the effect of most skills training does not last nor make any impact on the bottom line. The need for training is widely recognised but the difficulties of making it measurably effective are great. The implication is that sales managers are not providing the right climate for creativity to flourish. Furthermore, the way new techniques in marketing and promotional methods appear, it will be increasingly necessary for sales managers to initiate programmes to stimulate their sales teams to adopt a more creative approach to the development of sales from their territories and accounts.

Many managers have a poor understanding of motivation, and this prompts the search for simple solutions and explanations that unfortunately do not exist. The simple reality is that, unless some management action is taken to prevent it happening, new skills acquired in training deplete to vanishing point in a few short weeks.

Training also is narrowly focussed too often on product knowledge, reflecting the attitude that it is sufficient to find a good salesperson and provide the training for technical and product knowledge. In fact, the reverse is true. Salespeople with low skills and high product knowledge will nearly always under-perform compared with skilled salespeople with less than total product knowledge. Anyone who has been on the receiving end of boring salespeople droning on about the features of their products knows the truth of this.

Sales managers generally do not accept responsibility for training and development. There is a lack of field accompaniment, observation and coaching and a failure to identify real training needs. These criteria combined suggest that sales managers are not making enough effort to understand what truly makes their people tick and to provide the personal growth and development opportunities they need in their job. It is quite astonishing that, in spite of all the research in recent years, demonstrating time and again the crucial importance of skills such as questioning and listening, they still represent the most common skill deficiency.

SALES MANAGERS MUST BE ABLE TO MOTIVATE

What motivates salespeople is debatable. Kovach[68] in 1987 produced a paper that examined the results of previous research into employee motivation. The factors swung from 'the need for recognition' as the main motivator to 'having interesting work to do'. I favour the work carried out by Shipley and Keily[69] in the 1980s, which shows that salespeople are motivated by reward, recognition and achievement.

It could be seen as somewhat glib to say that your learning events (whether in a classroom or in the field) should be rewarding, that people should be recognised for having learned new skills and that they should gain a sense of achievement from your training programme, and yet this is exactly what is required.

The reward from your training programme is that salespeople will achieve more as a result of following your suggestions. Consequently, you should carry out a full and researched evaluation of the effect of your training. People who are seen to try out new skills on your programme should receive recognition. You should award prizes for the best presentations even if it is just a certificate. It is important that sales managers understand the importance of reward and recognition when training salespeople in the field. It is from these rewards and recognition that salespeople get a sense of achievement. Research in the 1950s showed that the highest level of human motivation comes from a sense of achievement and recent research reinforces these theories. Modern salespeople have different values from their 1950s counterparts, and achievement is derived from reward and recognition. The three are inexorably linked.

Winer and Schiff's research in 1980[70] found that salespeople placed a high priority on financial reward as a main motivating factor in job performance. Making more money was specified as an important

---

[68]   Kovach, K. (1987). What Motivates Employees?, *Business Horizons*, September.
[69]   Shipley, D. and Keily, J. (1988). 'Motivation and dissatisfaction of industrial salespeople', *European Journal of Marketing*, Vol. 22, No. 1.
[70]   Winer, L. and Schiff, J.S. (1980). 'Industrial salespeople's views on motivation', *Industrial Marketing Management*, Vol. 9, No.4, October.

motivator. Your training programme must be seen as a way of meeting these demands.

If reward is the primary motivating factor for salespeople, then you must link your training events accordingly by getting trainees to establish early on in the training event what it is they want from the sales job. Your training should be seen as a method of obtaining just that. Ultimately, sales trainers and sales managers have a joint responsibility to motivate people to want to learn. In order to do that, everyone needs to understand fully the problems faced from closed minds and negative attitudes. Somewhere along the line, in your role as a trainer and a sales manager, you need to create your own stories and analogies. They do not come from books or exist in other people's training notes. They come from experience, and especially experience of having been there yourself. Good sales trainers and sales managers have a history of success and of failure, and are prepared to share those experiences, especially with new starters.

Most managers still find the whole subject of how to motivate salespeople a complete mystery. Levinson's article[71] on the subject is particularly revealing. He says that motivational theory is hardly sparse and most executives have studied the subject in depth at some time or another:

> Many have taken part in managerial grid training, group dynamics laboratories, and seminars on the psychology of management, and a wide range of other forms of training. Some have run the full gamut of training experiences; others have embraced a variety of panaceas offered by quacks.

But as with skills training, he believes that the expectations of companies that their people will change after a training event, no matter how senior they are, is totally unrealistic and I could not agree more:

> Furthermore, it is one thing to become aware of one's feelings; it is quite another to do something different about managing them, let alone managing those forces that affect the feelings of

[71]   Levinson H. (1973). 'Asinine attitudes towards motivation, *Harvard Business Review*, Jan/Feb.

other people. Experience is not enough; training in a conceptual framework and supervised skill practice is also required.

In addition, far too many managers come from engineering, scientific, legal or financial backgrounds in which a heavy emphasis is placed on cognitive rationality and measurable verifiable facts. When these people become responsible for others, they tend to apply the same basic logic and expect others to do the same. Many simply cannot grasp the softer skills required of effective people managers.

Understanding motivation

Anderson, Hare and Bush reported in their book, *Professional Sales Management*,[72] that 85% of sales-forces were weakly motivated. They also said that companies spend large sums of resources in market research into buyer behaviour but next to nothing in researching how to motivate their own people.

As a result, sales managers generally rely upon a mixture of intuition, folklore, tradition, and other managers as role models for their own beliefs and practices with regard to motivation

Sales managers should understand that there is no one motivational factor that works in all cases. Instead, managers must have a broad knowledge of their subject so that they can adapt to any given situation. It should also be remembered that all motivation is in fact self-motivation. Salespeople cannot be motivated unless they decide to let themselves be motivated. Therefore, sales managers have the responsibility of creating the environment and incentives that encourage salespeople to want to motivate themselves.

Some researchers and some personnel departments may tell you that there is a distinct breed who make the most successful salespeople. And yet all the evidence indicates that sales forces tend to be a composite of personality types, motivated by a number of factors, non-financial as well as financial.

---

[72] Anderson, R.E., Hare, J.F. and Bush, A.J. (1988). *Professional Sales Management*, New York: McGraw Hill.

Using Maslow

I have earlier discussed Maslow's Theory of Motivation,[73] [74] which was a precursor to Frederick Herzberg's theory of Motivation and Management.[75] The same principles apply to motivational buying habits and to basic theory on motivating salespeople. It is worth considering however, that the motivational hierarchy described by Maslow may have differing interpretations and therefore applications between salespeople and sales managers. **Table 9** shows a comparison which might be useful when deliberating how to apply Maslow's theories.

	Salespeople	Sales managers
1	A salesperson must drive themselves in order to achieve results.	A manager must be careful not to drive people in order to achieve results.
2	A salesperson must be impatient and constantly be on the move.	A manager must let situations develop and ripen. A manager needs almost infinite patience.
3	Salespeople require constant recognition for the results they produce.	A manager must learn to give recognition and accept a secondary role in the process.
4	Salespeople must produce, they must get results.	The manager, whilst needing numbers, must take the longer view of business growth and personnel development.
5	Salespeople have to be self-reliant.	A manager must rely almost completely on others.
6	A salesperson is a doer. They need the action.	A sales manager is an organiser. They orchestrate the process. They rely on others to make things happen.
7	Salespeople must know themselves and must study how they work best.	A manager must be a student of others. They must constantly search for talent and accept people who operate completely differently from the way they do.
8	A salesperson builds loyalty with their customers.	A sales manager builds company loyalty.

[73] Maslow, A. (1954). *Motivation and Personality*, New York: Harper & Row.
[74] Maslow, A. (1943). 'A theory of human motivation', *Psychological Review*, Vol. 50.
[75] Herzberg, F., Mauser, B. and Snyderman, B. (1959). *The Motivation to Work*, Hoboken, NJ: John Wiley & Sons.

	Salespeople	Sales managers
9	Salespeople never give up. They believe everybody can be sold to given enough time and effort.	A sales manager must learn to cut losses quickly. They can invest just so much in a person and then something must change dramatically.
10	A salesperson can be nonconformist in order to produce results.	A manager must operate close to the book in order to succeed. They have far less freedom than salespeople, and they must operate effectively within constraints.

Table 9: Applying Maslow's Theory

Conclusions on motivation

Different people are motivated by different factors. It is very much a case of horses for courses. Sales managers should attempt to improve the performance of their people over a significant period of time. The most dramatic productivity gains are short-lived, yet long-term success is based on gradual improvements. There is a saying that 'success by the inch is a cinch, but by the yard is hard'.

It is also important for managers to recognise that, whilst one salesperson may see a pay rise in terms of what the money will buy, another may value it purely from a recognition point of view, and as a reward for superior performance. It is true also that senior salespeople are usually more productive as a result of money-related reward motivators, whereas junior people are more likely to be motivated by opportunity for advancement.

Sales managers need to be wary of adopting blanket motivational approaches, and concentrate more upon the individual. It may be a good idea to split your team up into the sort of groups that Mossien and Fram[76] suggest. They see the following four distinct groups of salespeople in any team:

- **The trainee group:** These new salespeople need constant stroking and training, and need to be in contact with the trainer regularly in the field.

- **Salespeople with some experience:** These need to be given the opportunity for continuing training in more advanced techniques,

---

[76] Mossien, H. and Fram, E.H. (1973). 'Segmentation of salesforce motivation', *Akron Business & Economic Review*, Winter.

such as behavioural studies. They may also be given different incentives.

- **Senior salespeople:** These need to be given the opportunity to communicate with middle management, and be involved more in the decision-making process, and attend special 'peer group' meetings.

- **Top salespeople:** These need to be able to talk to the top senior management of the company and take leadership roles in sales meetings. These are the people who should enjoy special benefits such as bonuses, luxury cars and expense accounts. They need regularly to be asked their opinion on the company's marketing policy and strategies.

Most recent research points to the incalculable value of non-standard rewards. The single most workable non-financial reward is recognition. All levels of people appreciate some form of public recognition.

Bill Kelley,[77] in *Sales and Marketing Management*, in 1986, suggested the following format for developing a recognition programme:

- **The programme should be objective and based on performance only:** It has to be clear to everybody why an individual won.

- **There should be no subjective judgements:** The easiest way to do this is to base all recognition programmes on results.

- **Everybody must have a chance to win:** It should neither be so difficult that no one will win, nor so easy, that everybody wins.

- **The award should be presented in public:** Much of the recognition is lost if there is no public ceremony, or if awards or certificates or plaques are sent out in the post.

- **The ceremony must be in good taste:** A poorly done recognition programme can leave people uninspired, and take away any motivation they may have had.

---

[77]   Kelley, B. (1986). 'Recognition reaps rewards', *Sales and Marketing Management*, June.

- **The programme must be highly publicised:** If nobody knows about it, or it is poorly communicated so that no one understands it, it will lack involvement. It must be promoted in company publications and be seen as an important part of the company's overall strategy.

SALESPEOPLE'S ATTITUDES TOWARDS MANAGEMENT

Now that you are on the ladder or are contemplating taking up management, you may have forgotten what you used to think about sales managers. When I was researching successful salespeople, one of the factors that surfaced regularly was their utter disdain for their line managers. Many successful salespeople have a personal sense of responsibility for their own success or failure and see little that managers contribute to either. Many successful salespeople have nothing good to say about their managers. In addition, the term 'team' only really has meaning for the manager. Successful salespeople have little time for 'teambuilding' activities.

An important truth for you to consider is that people learn from how their managers behave not from what they say.

Good and bad managers

When I facilitate training for sales managers, I usually conduct an exercise of self-awareness where I ask them to think about a manager they deemed to have been a poor manager. Then to consider what that manager did, said, and how they behaved, and lastly how it made the salesperson feel. The responses received have been:

Bad managers were:

- Never there.
- Unapproachable.
- Patronising.
- Apathetic.
- Selfish.
- Uncommunicative.

- Unpredictable.
- Inconsistent.
- Told lies.
- Only interested in results.
- A bully.
- A sexist.

Good managers:

- Listened to me.
- Had time for me.
- Showed empathy.
- Asked my opinion.
- Encouraged me.
- Gave both freedom and responsibility.
- Kept commitments.
- Gave firm guidelines and expectations.
- Approachable.
- Created a good atmosphere.
- Rewarded with praise and with money.
- Believed in me – I had no limits.

Unfortunately, there appear to be more poor managers than good managers and we tend to learn more from poor managers than from good managers. The reason is that poor management is easier to execute. It takes less time. Being a good manager is difficult. It requires hard work.

NEXT ...

- How could you improve your sales career without going into sales management?

CHAPTER 16
SET YOUR GOALS HIGH

SUMMARY

- Money is a by-product of success. This means that success is the cause and money is the effect. Do not chase after money.
- There is nothing wrong with making mistakes. Learn from them. But never make the same mistake twice. People who say they have never made a mistake, have never actually done anything.
- Never quit.

Lawrence & Kleiner[78] say that there are three types of people who play the game of life: the spectators, the losers, and the winners. They list 10 qualities of winners, five of which they say are attitudinal and five corresponding actions:

Attitudinal

- Positive self-expectancy.
- Positive self-motivation.
- Positive self-image.
- Positive self-direction.
- Positive self-control.

Corresponding actions

- Positive self-discipline.
- Positive self-esteem.

---

[78] Lawrence, T.L. and Kleiner, B.H. (1986). 'The key to successful goal achievement', *Journal of Management Development*, July.

- Positive self-dimension.
- Positive self-awareness.
- Positive self-projection.

On one level, it is difficult to disagree with any of these. They all look and sound reasonable, even though there appears to be some duplication. Self-expectancy, self-image, self-dimension, and self-awareness seem to be the same thing, as are self-motivation, self-direction, and self-control. In most journals to do with goal achievement, a great deal of emphasis is placed on similar lists. These are the 'soft' skills of goal achievement. They are easy to talk about, but very, very difficult to emulate. Some people are naturally fearful and have a low self-esteem. Simply saying that all goal achievers have high esteem misses the point and might actually not be true. This is especially true of selling.

I found that high achievers in sales teams are as insecure as low achievers, and in some cases, probably more so. It is not unusual to see all of the above qualities expounded as being requisite to a successful selling career, yet I have not met anyone who, after having read that these qualities were necessary, was able to acquire them simply be being aware of them.

It would be like knowing that to score 50 with one dart on a dartboard, you have to hit the bull's eye. Whether you do or not has nothing to do with attitude but with practice. Even luck can play a part.

Those of us who take an amateur interest in sports probably know the difference between luck and skill. There might have been times when you played snooker with friends when, for the most part, your score depended upon circumstance rather than design. Many of us can pot a red. Once in a while, we might pot a colour. The usual behaviour is then to nod sagely as we walk around the table to take the next shot, pretending that we had intentionally placed the cue ball in a position for the next shot, whereas the reality was down to divine providence. Yet you never see 'luck' in lists of goal achievers. The response is that achievers make their own luck, and there is a certain truth in that.

BELIEF IN YOUR ABILITY TO SUCCEED

You have to believe that you can succeed. W.D. Wintle's poem, *The Man Who Thinks He Can*, ends:

> Life's battles don't always go to the stronger or faster man, but sooner or later, the man who wins is the man who thinks he can.

If you think you cannot do it, then you will not. If you believe that you can, you will.

You probably know the story about the bumblebee. Aeronautically, it has been proven that the bumblebee cannot fly. The shape and weight of its body, together with the size and position of its wings, scientists say ensure that it is impossible for the bumblebee to take off, let alone sustain flight. The problem is that nobody told the bumblebee.

Sometimes you have to ignore those messages that keep flying around inside your head, which say, "You can't do it. Forget it – it's impossible. Be happy with what you've got. It will only end in tears. Better the devil you know ...". Where do all these messages come from? It is certain that they have nothing to do with the potential of your life but with the experience of somebody else. These childhood messages really can get in the way if you let them. Sometimes, the comments are said to you for purportedly the best of reasons – but they are destructive nevertheless. You can achieve many of the things you want to achieve if you set your mind to it and you plan the steps you have to take. Do not believe those people who say you can achieve anything you want. I might want to be King of England, the Premier Football League's top scorer, and have a number 1 record in the charts playing *Mr Tambourine Man*,[79] but I somehow don't think it's not going to happen.

People who are successful plan for the long journey, but it does have to have some reality attached to it. They know that success is not achieved in a day. Unfortunately we have grown up in the late

---

[79]   Bob Dylan composition.

20th and early 21st centuries where it seems to be important to achieve everything in 24 hours, and if you do not, you are a failure.

It's better to be a tortoise than a hare.[80] Sometimes the journey is a lot more rewarding than the destination. It is like driving on a motorway. Motorways are great for getting to places fast, but often offer poor scenery. Taking the back road might take a lot longer but you see a lot more, and usually end up being more relaxed, having accomplished more when you get there.

Your plan to succeed should involve taking in the scenery. When you put your plan to succeed together, ask yourself about the quality factor as much as the quantity. Is there somewhere in your plan to succeed that says something about the quality of life you want? You probably know a lot of people who on the surface seem to have everything, and yet in their eyes, they have very little. Getting everything you want is of no use if along the journey you did some things you are none too proud of. Succeeding is important – but not at any cost.

There are all sorts of things you can do to succeed. You can cheat; you can lie; you can take substances to enhance your performance. You can cut someone up on the track and what for? Part of your plan has to be "I want to look at myself in the mirror and feel good about what I see". The single most important factor in your plan to succeed is a commitment to look after your name. It is all you have got to start out with and it is all you will end up with. Guard it jealously. Ask yourself when you are putting your plan together "How will this affect my name? Will this action enhance it or put my name in jeopardy? Will I be proud to pass that name on to my children? How comfortable will I be with my name in lights?" Look after your name. It is what will make you, and it is what can break you.

---

[80]   http://en.wikipedia.org/wiki/The_Tortoise_and_the_Hare

TAKING RESPONSIBILITY

Life for most people in selling is about the achievement of targets. Pesce[81] defines a goal as "… an objective or target expected to be reached within a fixed date; should be written down, measurable, and reviewed regularly".

Either your manager sets the target, or you had a hand in it, but whichever way it is put together, it has nothing to do with goals. Goals are something else altogether. The achievement of targets may contribute towards a goal, but on their own, targets are more to do with the things that benefit someone else – your manager or the company. There is nothing wrong with that, as after all, the Piper calls the tune. Targets can be an important function of goal achievement, but they should not be confused with goals. Also it is important to have more than one goal. Not so many as to make it confusing, but enough to keep you going. It is important to plant a number of seeds in your goal garden. Some of them just will not grow – and if you spend a lifetime waiting for one seed to grow and it does not, and you have nothing else to look forward to, you could become disillusioned. I have met a lot of people in the later stages of their lives who seemed only to have had one goal, and when they failed to achieve it, they looked back and saw a wasted life, from which they were cynically drifting into the future.

We all need goals and life is all about goals. Look in any street where children are kicking a ball. It is not long before either a couple of coats or sweaters are placed on the ground, or a goal chalked up on a wall. Just kicking a ball around is not much fun without an aim – a goal. Unfortunately for many people, life is a bit like kicking a ball around without an end result, and the process is about as satisfying.

Within everybody, there exists the opportunity for achievement. Too many people neither set goals nor experience achievement. Some blame the environment, some their parents, some blame politicians and some even the weather. In reality, the answer to goal achievement is looking straight at you in the mirror every morning.

---

[81] Pesce, V. (1989). *A Complete Manual of Professional Selling*, Upper Saddle River, NJ: Prentice Hall.

The first lesson to learn about the achievement of goals is that you are responsible.

As the 21st century unfolds, that is a hard lesson to learn. We have been brought up to expect that other people are responsible for the way things are, and in many ways, conditioned to believe that it is not our fault in underachievement, but T-H-E-M. There are no such people as THEM. Achieving goals, doing something with your life, is your responsibility. It is amazing how many people spend more time and energy plotting the course of their holidays than in determining the course of their lives. What is more important – the two weeks on the Costa del Sol, the trip to Florida, the world cruise – or the rest of your life? And yet for vast numbers of people, the planning and preparation that goes into a) deciding where to go on holidays and b) how to get there far outstrips deciding the course of their lives, and how to get there. If you do not know where you are going, do not be amazed when you end up somewhere else.

ONE STEP AT A TIME

Salespeople do not deliberately plan to fail. However many do fail to plan. The fact is that failure can be avoided and success achieved, and that you can plan for success. Samuel Smiles[82] said:

> It is not eminent talent that is required to ensure success in any pursuit so much as purpose – not merely power to achieve but the will to labour energetically and perseveringly.

His book is a treasure trove of examples of people, ordinary people, who reached the zenith of achievement – not because they were the most talented or had the luckiest breaks, but because they had purpose, determination, and a plan – a plan to succeed.

The trick is in understanding that the energy required, and the plans that have to be laid, are not great, just more than the next person's. The difference between the words 'ordinary' and 'extraordinary' is the little word 'extra'. In order to be successful, and

---

[82]   Smiles, S. (1986). *Self Help*, Harmondsworth: Penguin.

as part of your plan to be successful in life, you need to do that little bit extra.

Winners understand that, without a plan, without a decision to win in the first place, then the playing field is level – then you have to rely on luck. I do not know about you but I do not want the course of my life to rely on luck.

George Bernard Shaw said:

> The people who get on in this world are the people who get up and look for the circumstances they want, and if they can't find them, make them.

I believe people make their own luck – good and bad. Without a plan, your life is like a ship without a rudder. You will end up where time and tide will take you.

The problem is that, for most of us, getting through each day is enough. For those of you with young children who seem to take up your every waking hour, or a demanding job, or the 1,001 other things that fill up your lives, it can be a real effort sometimes even to consider where it is your life is going, and whether you are happy with the course of it.

Actually, planning where you want your life to go at times can seem impossible, when in fact the reality is somewhat different. The Chinese say that a journey of 1,000 miles begins with the first step. The journey of the rest of your life also is made up of small steps and small events. Whether you realise it, you are constantly in the process of changing both physically and mentally. You cannot stop your body ageing, and neither can you stop your mind from acquiring new stimuli. It is what you do with the stimuli that determines whether your life will change for the better.

Success by the inch is a cinch; by the yard it's hard. Trying to do too much at once is bound to fail – it is too much to take on. Take things one step at a time. All you have to do is to move forward.

I have heard people say, "I couldn't run a marathon". Of course you could, if you did it a step at a time. It might take you a year to complete, but that is not the point.

It is no good looking back at life thinking, "I wish"' or "I could have". Do not wish and then not be prepared to do something about it. Always take the first step. The first step in planning to succeed is to take the first step. Working out how to achieve a goal means deciding what the first step is, and once you have done that, you can take the first step. It is absolutely certain that without taking the first step, you will not achieve your goal. If you do not run the first mile, there is no chance of winning the marathon. If you do not draft the letter applying for the job, you will not get it. If you fail to telephone the customer for the appointment, you certainly will not make the sale, and your goal of being number one will not happen.

People who are goal achievers do not do it in one go. You cannot write a book in one sitting. The chances are strongly against becoming rich and famous in 24 hours, and yet some people seem to believe that that is what happens. Goal achievers make it look easy because you only see the end result – you were not around to count all the many little steps it took.

Life has taught us to stand at the winning line to watch winners. Nobody stands at the start line. The winners do, though. They know that winning is all about starting. To achieve a goal, you have to make a start. Take the first step. Decide what you want to do and take the first step.

PAYING THE PRICE

The other thing about the achievement of goals is that it does not come free. Other people's goals and other people's achievements look easy until you realise that there is a price to be paid, and you might not like the price. Everything looks alright in the window until you see the price tag. Everything in life is on sale. The difference between goal achievers and non-goal achievers is that the achievers decide to pay the price.

Deciding what you want to do, and making the first step, will bring you face to face with the price tag. It is at this point where you have to ask yourself, "Is it really what I want to do?" Put the picture in your mind of having achieved the goal, and ask yourself, "Am I prepared to pay this price for this goal?"

It is at this stage that 95% of people will hum and hah about the price, and either decide to think about it or decide against it – in fact, they are both the same. If a goal has to be thought about, it is not a goal – it is just a whim. A true goal should scream out at you, "I am a goal and price doesn't matter". You see, the price of not achieving a goal in fact may be much greater. The price for not setting goals or even attempting to achieve something in your life could be realising it when it is too late. For some goals, you might run out of time, and there is nothing worse than saying, "If only ...".

Having said that, setting out on the journey is almost as good as getting there. There is a saying that success is about the journey and not the destination. Too much focus on the destination can cause you to lose sight of the treasures on the journey. That is an important lesson, too. The journey towards a goal can be more exciting than the goal itself. You can learn so much about yourself on the way to achieving a goal that sometimes the goal itself does not matter anymore, but the activity of goal achievement in itself becomes the goal. Doing something to shape the course of your life, in itself, will make you a better person, and will separate you from the great mass of people whose lives are shaped by others. It has been said that life is the pursuit of happiness whereas I believe that life is the happiness of pursuit. It is important you understand that, and perhaps it is something that you will not learn until it happens to you.

By taking the first step, and by focusing on what you can achieve now, you will start having small successes. Big successes are always as a result and consequence of smaller successes. Weight-lifters start with smaller weights first. Show jumpers do not attempt a six-foot wall straight away. Writers begin each novel with a first page.

What is important is to experience success. Once you feel the exhilaration of your first small success, you will want more. Part of your plan to succeed has to be to get some small successes first.

In the world of selling, the opportunities for small successes are all around you. Telephoning for an appointment is a small success, but without it you will never achieve the big one. Getting agreement from your customer that it is worth gathering some facts about them, or their business, is a small success. Getting a second appointment is a small success. Reaching agreement that your customers have unfulfilled needs is a small success. Agreeing to do something about it is a small success. Identifying other people, whom your customer knows have similar needs, is a small success. Getting your customers to introduce you to their acquaintances is a small success. In total, they all add up to what the job is all about simply by taking it a step at a time.

The important thing is to focus on it in the here and now, and a step at a time. Your plan may say where it is you want to go, but unless you concentrate on it a step at a time, you might drive off the road because you were concentrating on the horizon, and failed to see the turn in the road. Your plan to succeed has to deal with the here and now. Having decided where it is you want to go, you have to decide how to do it. This action alone will guarantee that you will achieve more in two years than most people achieve in 20 years. People have a tendency to look at the whole journey, and it puts them off.

WRITE DOWN YOUR GOALS

Whatever your goals are, the important thing is to write them down. Do not restrict yourself in the early stages of writing down your goals. Do not make any judgements about the worth or likelihood of a particular goal, just write them all down until you cannot think of any more.

Ask yourself "What do I want to do with my life? (Forget the things that you think are stopping you). Who would I like to be? What sort of person do I want to be? What sort of job do I want? Where do I want to live? How much money do I want to earn?"

When you have your list of goals, check that they are specific, and if some are not, then you should make them so. If you have written down a holiday of a lifetime, say where it is you want to go, and for how long. Be specific about how you want to get there, and what you want to do when you get there. Will somebody be going with you, and will you be paying for him or her? Will they want to go? What is the reason for the goal? Is it just something that everybody else does, or is it something that you really want to do? This process of focusing on the importance of the goals, and the steps of specifying the parameters exactly will give you some ideas about the likelihood of achieving that goal, and how to go about it.

Writing down each of your goals gives it some airing of the sort that will help you to decide whether it really is something you want to do or not, and more importantly, what you intend to do about it. You may end up with 20 or 30 goals, and that is OK, but you will have to draw out of these a list on a separate bit of paper at least three, and no more than, five primary goals. These three to five goals become the things that you will concentrate on. This is the destination.

Now put some time-scales on them, and work out the steps you have to take. Then do it. Take the first step. You will be amazed how much you can achieve. Do it. Write down your goals. Be specific. Ask yourself why you want a particular goal.

It can often be helpful to construct some kind of goal-setting plan, as this can facilitate the breaking-down of your goals into smaller, more realistic tasks. The plan should include:

- Goals to be realised.
- Actions that need to be taken in order to realise each goal.
- Hurdles that need to be overcome.
- Date you plan to start/finish each task.
- Personal rewards after realising each goal.

More than anything, you must possess the self-belief and desire to achieve these goals, despite any obstacles that you may have to overcome. If you have a clear picture in your mind of what you want to achieve, then this will make your goal much easier to realise.

You should include goals that cover all the different parts of your life, not just your career. A clearly written plan of what you want to do, and how you are going to do it, is essential; houses are never built without blueprints.

Life can become mundane if you have nothing to strive for. Goal-setting can relieve the frustration and help you to make your life better in the long run.

Grant a certain amount of flexibility for your long-term goals, as your views can change as time passes. It is hard to predict exactly where you will be in the years to come, but it is possible to influence the direction in which you are going.

When you have become used to the process of goal-setting, then you can apply this to areas of your life other than work, such as personal, domestic and family goals. As before, writing then down can make them seem a whole lot more realistic and possible. If you do not get into the habit of writing your goals down, then they may never come into fruition. Unwritten goals are merely daydreams.

You must have a specific hold on what it is that you want. Vague wishes are not achievable goals. Goals must be ambitious. To achieve your goal, you must have to do something that will make you perform better than you have ever done in the past. If not, then you will not find ways of improving your performance in the future.

Ensure that there is some degree of symmetry between your short and long-term goals. If you are constantly striving towards an unforeseeable future, then this may become difficult as time passes.

There is nothing mysterious or difficult about success. Success is simply doing a few simple things, and doing them well. The horse that comes in first in a race wins a prize 20 times the value of the horse that comes in second, though the winner does not run 20 times faster than the second horse. This is also true of life. To earn 20 times as much money as the next person, we do not have to work 20 times as hard, we simply have to be a nose ahead.

WINNING AND LOSING

And yet – is that what it all comes down to – winning or losing? It really depends on what it is you are trying to achieve. If it is only ever about winning – you might be disappointed. I am not saying it is good to lose – but it does sometimes help to have lost – if only to feel what it is like. My experience tells me that if you have never lost, then chances are it will happen at some time. For those of you considering a career in sales management, losing is as valuable an experience as winning.

Last, remember life, and a career as a professional salesperson, is a journey not a destination.

NEXT ...

- What do you want to be? What do you like? What do you dislike? (If you dislike it, you will not be any good at it). What do you need to do? When are you going to start?

- What do you want to happen in the short term (maximum one year), medium term (2 to 3 years), and long term (10 years plus)?

- If you won the lottery tomorrow, what job would you do for the rest of your life? Find a way to move towards it because that is what you really want to do and you will be more fulfilled moving towards it than never starting the journey.

ABOUT THE AUTHOR

Frank Salisbury is Chairman of the Business & Training Solutions International Group, the Institute of Commercial Management Chief Examiner for Sales & Marketing, and Joint Founder of the Institute of Professional Selling and the International College of Professional Selling. Frank is a leading expert on the subject of Sales, Sales Leadership, and Sales Coaching.

He has designed and delivered a significant range of personal development programmes for individuals and organisations aimed at helping salespeople achieve their potential. These programmes, and this book, have drawn on Frank's research into performance improvement processes in sports, music, acting and dance, and how these could be applied in the world of sales.

He has spoken at numerous sales conferences and seminars where his style has received acclaim from those who hear him speak with a passion for life and achievement.

Frank lives in the North East of England with his wife Pauline. He is a life-long fan of Newcastle United, who he says he has supported through thin and thin. His previous books include:

- *Coaching Champions: How to Build a Winning Sales Team*, 2nd edition, Oak Tree Press, Cork, 2011.

- *Coaching Champions: How to Get the Best Out of Your Salespeople*, Oak Tree Press, Dublin, 2001 (co-authored with Karl O'Connor and Cariona Neary).

- *Sales Training*: Second Edition, Gower, 1998 (seen as the 'bible' for sales trainers).

- *Developing Managers as Coaches*, McGraw-Hill, 1996.

- *Sales Training*, McGraw-Hill, 1992.

OAK TREE PRESS

Oak Tree Press develops and delivers information, advice and resources for entrepreneurs and managers. It is Ireland's leading business book publisher, with an unrivalled reputation for quality titles across business, management, HR, law, marketing and enterprise topics. NuBooks is its recently-launched imprint, publishing short, focused ebooks for busy entrepreneurs and managers.

In addition, through its founder and managing director, Brian O'Kane, Oak Tree Press occupies a unique position in start-up and small business support in Ireland through its standard-setting titles, as well as training courses, mentoring and advisory services.

Oak Tree Press is comfortable across a range of communication media – print, web and training, focusing always on the effective communication of business information.

Oak Tree Press, 19 Rutland Street, Cork, Ireland.

T: + 353 21 4313855 F: + 353 21 4313496.

E: info@oaktreepress.com W: www.oaktreepress.com.

Lightning Source UK Ltd.
Milton Keynes UK
UKOW020129291011

181101UK00001B/12/P